M000206181

HOPE
after SUICIDE

ONE WOMAN'S JOURNEY
from DARKNESS
TO LIGHT

HOPE
after SUICIDE

ONE WOMAN'S JOURNEY
from DARKNESS
TO LIGHT

WENDY PARMLEY

PLAIN SIGHT PUBLISHING
AN IMPRINT OF CEDAR FORT, INC.
SPRINGVILLE, UT

© 2014 Wendy Parmley
All rights reserved.

No part of this book may be reproduced in any form whatsoever, whether by graphic, visual, electronic, film, microfilm, tape recording, or any other means, without prior written permission of the publisher, except in the case of brief passages embodied in critical reviews and articles.

This is not an official publication of The Church of Jesus Christ of Latter-day Saints. The opinions and views expressed herein belong solely to the author and do not necessarily represent the opinions or views of Cedar Fort, Inc. Permission for the use of sources, graphics, and photos is also solely the responsibility of the author.

"Angel Lullaby" lyrics by Carol Lynn Pearson, *My Turn on Earth*, reprinted with permission.

ISBN 13: 978-1-4621-1500-6

Published by Plain Sight Publishing, an imprint of Cedar Fort, Inc.
2373 W. 700 S., Springville, UT, 84663
Distributed by Cedar Fort, Inc., www.cedarfort.com

LIBRARY OF CONGRESS CATALOGING-IN-PUBLICATION DATA

Parmley, Wendy, 1962- author.
  Hope after suicide / Wendy Parmley.
      pages cm
  Wendy Parmley recounts her healing after her mother's suicide.
  Includes bibliographical references and index.
  ISBN 978-1-4621-1500-6 (alk. paper)
  1. Suicide. 2. Suicide victims--Family relationships. 3. Grief. 4. Parmley, Wendy, 1962- I. Title.

HV6545.P238 2014
362.28'4092--dc23
[B]

                        2014017493

Cover design by Angela D. Baxter
Cover design © 2014 by Lyle Mortimer
Edited and typeset by Daniel Friend

Printed in the United States of America

10 9 8 7 6 5 4 3 2 1

Printed on acid-free paper

Dedicated to Dad, who taught me perseverance despite challenge, deep loyalty to family, faith in God, and hope in a Savior who can make all things right.

Praise for

HOPE AFTER SUICIDE

Hope after Suicide *is a beautifully written account of one woman's journey from devastation to hope and healing. The author's account of her healing journey . . . is inspiring and empowering. The book encourages the reader to embrace life again after a loved one's suicide with love, forgiveness, and a new sense of hope.*
> —Lisa Bullock, intuitive coach at The Crystal Haven and suicide survivor

Parmley's powerful personal journey of healing from her young mother's suicide is a truly inspirational example of . . . the essential truths of the difficult, far-reaching work that must be done to overcome . . . deep, scarring, personal emotional pain. Her willingness to share her journey . . . is a welcome testament that one's darkness truly can become light.
> —Aaron F. Gardner, MAC, LCMHC, practicing psychotherapist

Wendy's book is both the storm and the ensuing calm. To those who have treaded this path, its words represent a hard-fought triumph over an incomprehensible tragedy. To all of us, her experience is a touching reminder of God's great capacity to understand the desires and intentions of one's heart and the overarching comprehensiveness of the Savior's Atonement.
> —James L. Snyder, PhD, clinical neuropsychologist

Enduring the pain of losing a loved on is one of life's most difficult trials. When that loss comes because of suicide, the pain and grief take on an entirely different persona. In her book, Wendy Parmley opens her heart to share her own story of loss to suicide. . . . There is something for everyone to relate to and to learn from in this beautifully told story of . . . a woman . . . trying to make peace with the past and the present.
> —Melissa Pahl, nurse educator

Wendy Parmley is a gifted writer who can bring the reader through the feelings of despair, loneliness, and sadness of suicide and then give the reader the feeling of hope and peace that can occur for those who suffer. I highly recommend this book to all who want healing or understanding.

—Janelle Stopa, Orem, Utah

We all have secrets of some sort, and Wendy Parmley has bravely shared a very private one in this book. In doing so, she lends courage to those of us who are wrestling with our own pasts. Her writing is engaging and fresh . . . her journey to face her past can give readers hope for their own healing. I loved this book and am better for having read it.

—Jennifer Pollei, Orem, Utah

Wendy Parmley tells this powerful story with courage and grace.

—Jackie Clegg Dodd, wife of former US Senator Chris Dodd

Contents

Prologue

I'd better hurry," I thought, looking at the clock. It was 6:45 a.m.—only fifteen minutes before I was to meet Marie at the gas station between our two homes to begin our ride up the canyon.

Marie and I had just begun cycling together that summer. She had been riding for a few years and sailed with ease on her sleek road bike. She was patient and encouraging while I pedaled my heavy store-brand mountain bike beside her.

My younger sister had grown into a beautiful woman who gave her life in service to others—her family, her friends, and her church—and she willingly shared her healing gifts with those closest to her. I looked forward to our morning rides. They were the times we could talk like sisters can about our present headaches and past pains. Marie shared her wisdom and her heart with me.

"I don't know why," I told her that morning, "but I am so out of breath. It seems like my heart won't beat fast enough."

Riding on the paved trail, we were just coming to the sharp bend that would take us under the overpass and next to the river as we began our mountain climb.

"We'll want to move single file into the right-hand lane when we go around this curve," Marie said. She told me about a tragic accident just a few weeks earlier. An older gentleman walking up the canyon had been hit head-on by a cycler who couldn't see around the blind corner. The man was still in a coma.

I moved behind Marie as we turned the corner, and my front tire clipped her back tire. I lost control, and in seeming slow motion, I fell

1

with my heavy bike to the left of the paved trail, my head landing on the bottom rail of the riverside fence. I felt an electric current surge through my body. I knew I had hit the back of my head below my helmet. My nephew had died following a seemingly benign hit to the back of his head while skateboarding, and I begged Marie not to let me die.

Marie held my bleeding head in her lap. "Wendy, look at me. Focus here. You are not going to die," she said calmly, trying to quiet my panicked fears while we waited for the ambulance.

"Mommy," I cried.

I forced myself to stay awake as the world seemed to darken. *Don't close your eyes, Wendy,* I said to myself, fighting the urge to drift off to sleep.

Marie followed me to the hospital and sat by my side, urging the nurse to clean the blood from my head and face.

Over the next several weeks, I sat quietly on my back porch, hoping that the last autumn rays would heal my concussed brain and quiet the constant vibration that flowed through my body and the confusion that jumped in my brain.

Marie offered her healing gifts—craniosacral massage. As she held my head in her hands, light entered my body. I felt Mom just above my head, assisting Marie as she tried to remove the darkness and restore balance to my brain, which Marie described as a fish swimming in circles with only one fin.

In that quiet moment, Mom embraced my heart, and I knew that if I were to open my eyes, I would see her.

Although Marie's massage helped quiet my jumpy brain for a moment, as soon as I stood up again, my world was dizzy. Besides severe pain, I suffered constant nausea, my balance was poor, my eyes jumped from place to place on a page when I tried to read, and writing was difficult. Every noise was amplified a hundredfold, and the lights were blinding. My neuropsychologist described my brain like a shaken snow globe with all the sparkly specks swirling in constant motion. I couldn't will my brain to think.

With my darkened mind, I was unable to return to work. *If I can't work, then who am I? What good am I?* Between speech and balance and physical therapies, I lay on my bed and prayed for healing. But I slipped deeper into a depression. My world became darker.

"Mom, I get it now," I sobbed. "I get it!"

I couldn't turn on the lights in my jumbled brain, and I wished to be removed from this world. But Mom whispered in my ear and asked me to look—look with my heart and not with my mind. And she guided me on a journey to share her story. To share the story of my angel mom.

With my brain still dark, I looked back nearly forty years and saw my childhood. I saw my brand-new neighborhood with the brand-new split-level homes all lined in a perfect row that led up the long hill to the base of the mountain. I saw kids playing in the streets that divided the houses. I saw them riding their bikes in fields that would soon be transformed into more perfect new homes while their moms baked dinner and their dads worked. The perfect neighborhood in the middle of the perfect town—"Happy Valley."

At the end of the perfect week, I saw these neighbors leave for weekend camping trips while we pulled out our boat to go water-ski in the summer sun. When all the playing was done, we took our baths and cleaned our house and readied ourselves for the perfect Sabbath.

On Sunday mornings, we dressed in our best and filed down the hill with all the other neighbors and entered the sacred chapel to worship God with these friends.

The Mormon pastor, or *bishop*, as we called him, presided over this little flock of neighbors—the Mormon congregation called a *ward*. And my dad, a counselor or advisor to the bishop, sat next to him on the stand.

We partook of broken bread and of water in remembrance of a Savior who we were told could wash away all our sins. But surely none of my neighbors had sins—they all lived in perfect houses that looked just like mine and wore perfectly pressed clothes to this perfect little church at the bottom of the hill.

It doesn't matter that this was a Mormon community in "Happy Valley"; it could be any community where we put on masks and hide the truth, where we close the shades of our perfect little homes and turn out the lights so that no one can see.

Now, with my brain darkened and the lights dimmed, my angel mom nudged me. In the middle of the night, she lit a candle in my heart.

"Tell the story," she whispered.

So I picked up my pencil and began to write.

1

And the Day Turned into Night

Oh my God, Linda!" I woke with a start to my dad's frantic cries. Unaware of anything or anyone else, I bolted up the three flights of stairs from my basement bedroom to the top floor of our split-level home. There I found my dad with terror in his eyes, pacing back and forth, trapped in the too-small hallway. His hair disheveled and his muscles taut, Dad was unrecognizable as he screamed and cried, erratically running from room to room, ready to pounce on an unseen attacker.

My face felt hot, but my body felt cold; I was sick to my stomach, and my heart pounded in my throat. I felt the terror I saw in my dad. He seemed possessed by a darkness that would kill him if he didn't run away, and it frightened me. That fear would last nearly a lifetime—a fear I tried to suppress because Dad needed me.

"Wendy, watch the kids," he managed to say. "And whatever you do, don't go in the bathroom. Don't let anyone in the bathroom!" With those instructions, Dad, still in his silky navy-blue pajamas and bare feet, ran down the stairs and out the door. Escaping.

I was twelve years old—the oldest of five children. I was my mom's

5

right arm, and I babysat my younger brothers and sisters often. Now, with Dad running away like a crazy man, I was in charge.

Until this point, I hadn't noticed my younger siblings. My ten-year-old brother, Cary, seven-year-old sister, Marie, and four-year-old brother, Drew, had all awoken to my dad's cries and had gathered on the stairs that led to the closed bathroom door. My baby sister, Annie, crying in her crib across the hallway from the bathroom, seemed to know that something terrible had happened. I picked up Annie to comfort her and sat with her in my lap on the top stair to guard the bathroom door. Annie was barely one year old—chubby, lively, and wearing a ready, dimpled smile—but not *this* morning.

Cary put his hand on the bathroom door handle. It was locked but could easily be picked. "Cary, don't open it," I cautioned. Usually Cary had a mind of his own, and my warning would not have deterred him. But this time was different—we both were afraid of what lay behind that door.

On most other days, Cary was my companion in crime. We ran and played all summer in the foothills above our home. I still remember watching Cary carefully pull the legs off a frog he caught in the water dyke as he explained, "These are a delicacy to eat." He was twenty months younger, but he was bigger than I was—and more daring. We rode motorcycles together in those same foothills, and even though Cary wasn't quite eleven, he would jet up the side of the mountain and dare me to keep up. I felt like I could fly when I was with Cary.

Marie was born on the exact same day as Cary—just three years later. She was a darling towhead blonde with big blue eyes, and she was full of energy and life and sunshine. Although she hated standing still for pictures, she loved performing. She would sing and dance and spread her angel wings in our annual family Christmas pageant. She was a favorite of all the older couples in our neighborhood—she would knock on doors to visit them, and they would happily invite her in for a treat.

My kid brother Drew's hair was nearly as blond as Marie's, but his mischievous eyes were golden-brown like Mom's and matched the freckles on his nose. Drew won everyone's heart with his teasing, fun personality—running around playing cowboys and Indians or riding away on his big-wheel tricycle so you couldn't catch him. He was definitely a handful. Now he was crying, looking to me for answers that I didn't have. I was twelve. And I was terrified.

Annie cried in my lap, and although I was like her second mom, I couldn't quiet her. I wondered what was behind that door. I wanted to open it too, but no, I wouldn't. I couldn't. Dad said not to. So instead, I balanced Annie next to me, placed my cheek on the floor, and looked through the narrow space under the door. *Are those feet? Is she . . . ?* I couldn't be sure what I saw. My mind played tricks on me. I jolted upright and snatched Annie to my lap again. Panic swirled in my head, and a drum beat in my chest, ready for war. I couldn't think things through. I wanted to scream or cry or run away myself, but Dad had put me in charge with a strict command—"Don't go in the bathroom!"

I sat frozen on the top stair next to the closed bathroom door, the children's cries muffled by my racing thoughts and pounding heart. Breathing heavily, I didn't hear my dad return. He had run to our bishop's home on that cool early morning, hysterically wailing as he begged for them to open their front door with his fists. Marjean, the bishop's wife, described to me years later that his sobs were so loud she thought he was laughing. After learning what had happened and trying to quiet my barefoot dad, Marjean and the bishop quickly dressed themselves and accompanied Dad to our home.

Marjean came quietly up the stairs and skillfully took Annie from my arms as only an experienced mother could. Marjean had three daughters—the same ages as me, Cary, and Marie—and she seemed to know exactly what we needed. She gathered all the children to the living room at the bottom of the stairs.

I sat on the green-and-pink flowered, velvety couch with the matching hot-pink velvet chairs—the same couch my thirty-one-year-old mom had lain on each day after her cardiac arrest six months earlier. She was too weak to do her routine household chores, so she would lie there on her pillow and talk with me about my day when I got home from school. From that couch she would supervise us kids, making sure we completed our daily chores.

It was on that green and pink velvety couch just a couple months earlier that I sat next to Mom as she told me about the miscarriage. She explained that she felt a tumor growing inside her uterus—cancer—and Annie would probably be her last baby. I wrote in my diary about that day:

> *Mom told me that the baby is dead inside of her and that something else was growing inside of her and that she was going to have to have an*

operation. I thought to myself that if Annie is our last baby, I'm going to have the biggest family ever. I wonder if she will be.

Now I was sitting in that sacred spot—made holy by my mom's daily presence and the love she shared with me from it. My head was dizzy and my eyes were blurry as I heard Dad say—or was it the bishop? I couldn't be sure—as I heard someone say, "Mom is dead."

All the blood drained from my face as I sat there—speechless, lifeless, dead. I couldn't move. I couldn't breathe. I couldn't be. How could I go on without my mom?

2

One Last Kiss

Wendy and Jackie, come on, it's time to go," Mom said impatiently. "It's getting late, and we need to get Jackie home."

I was still chattering away with my friends after the church play. My favorite cousin, Jackie, had come all the way from the neighboring city to see the much-anticipated debut—and closing night—of the play that my favorite aunt, Cheri, directed. I had a starring role and was still flying high after the closing applause.

Jackie and I looked like twins. We both had blue eyes topped with bushy black eyebrows, big smiles, lots of energy, and long, messy blonde hair—that is, until seventh grade when Mom took me to a professional stylist. She cut my hair off right before my eyes as I sat dumbfounded looking at myself in the big mirror. Until then, the only way you could tell Jackie and me apart was by my glasses. In fact, Jackie would sometimes wear those ugly gold-framed glasses so we could play tricks on our aunts and uncles and try to confuse them. We were either really good at the deception or else they just played along. Either way, those were good times. The best times!

At the moment, Jackie and I were talking with Brad and Brad—the freckled-face, redheaded Brad who lived next door, and the cuter, brown-haired, well-built, eighth-grade Brad who lived around the block. Cute Brad was the police chief's son, and both Jackie and I had a crush on him, but, of course, he liked Jackie. Jackie always seemed so confident. She was a natural with the guys. Tonight was no different. Although I was secretly jealous, I acted sure of myself and flirted even more when Jackie was around, trying to keep up.

9

"Wendy, *now*," Mom said with emphasis. "It's time to go!" Mom carried Annie on her hip and came toward us like she meant business. She was only five-foot-two, but she could cover ground fast. And she was coming straight for us.

Although Mom was strikingly beautiful, she was what you could call a tomboy. She was great at sports and very competitive. She taught all her kids how to Indian leg-wrestle. Of course, she always won. Even Dad didn't stand a chance against Mom even though he was nearly a whole foot taller.

Mom loved the outdoors, especially the mountain haven where we rode horses and motorcycles and snowmobiles. We played softball, swam in the river, and collected wild peppermint leaves and watercress. Mom tried to convince us that you could have a sandwich made just from watercress leaves. If you put enough mayonnaise and salt on it, it almost became edible. I'm sure it helped us grow a few more inches, though, and Mom was convinced that these herbs had all sorts of natural vitamins that would help us live forever.

We spent an entire summer at Mom's haven one year, washing our clothes on a washboard and gathering wood for the fire pit where we roasted hotdogs and marshmallows. We learned lessons that summer that could only be taught in God's great outdoor classroom.

Mom filled our home with life and love and laughter. She canned peaches, baked whole wheat bread, and grew sprouts to add to the salads she tried to feed us every day. Although I didn't much care for the salads, I loved to spread a heaping spoon of peanut butter on hot bread fresh from the oven, then top it with raw honey that, even though it was so crystallized in the honey jug that you had to dig it out, would melt and slide off the peanut butter as soon as you slathered it on. My favorite after-school treats, though, were graham crackers dipped in milk. In seventh grade, I got home earlier than the other children and got to have Mom all to myself for a few minutes if Annie was taking a nap. She loved teaching me how to dip the crackers just right and eat peanut butter straight from the jar—you just had to make sure the milk was right there so your throat didn't get stuck shut.

My mom was a health nut, and she dragged me to all sorts of classes that taught us how to live to be a hundred. She even took me to the local health spa, where we sat in the sauna, breathing in eucalyptus to cleanse our sinuses and sweating out toxins from our pores. Just when

I thought I would die from heat exhaustion, she coaxed me into the ice plunge—a pool of water with actual ice cubes in it. I thought I would have a heart attack!

Although she was very health conscious, Mom had a sweet tooth. I loved sneaking with her to the Hostess outlet. It was like a covert operation. We would fill the cart to overflowing with Twinkies, Ding-Dongs, lemon pies, and coconut-covered Snowballs. We even snagged an occasional loaf of white bread for an extra treat. Once home, we'd stash the treats where no one else would find them and take them out when no one was looking. It was our secret.

Mom was everyone's best friend and confidant. Her bubbly, magnetic personality drew people to her. They trusted her with their secrets and looked to her for health advice. She took quilts to new moms and casseroles to old ladies. She was always on the phone, laughing and giggling with her high school girlfriends or one of her four older sisters, all the while pulling the cord through the house while she kept busy cleaning.

Mom was a meticulous homemaker. She taught us to dust and vacuum, do the dishes, and scrub toilets. She was very particular in her work and taught me to get down eye-level with the kitchen counter to make sure every last crumb had been wiped away. You could say she was a perfectionist—and I thought she *was* perfect.

But right now she was mad—or was she just tired? Mom didn't get mad very often, but this time I knew she meant business. "Come on, Jackie, we'd better go," I said reluctantly as we walked toward Mom. "Bye, guys!" Jackie hollered over her shoulder, her hair flipping behind her.

Mom led the way through the dark parking lot to our orange VW bus. It was a stick shift, and although I was only twelve, Mom taught me how to shift so she could nurse the baby while she drove. It was getting late, though, and Mom put Annie in her infant seat while Jackie and I climbed in the back.

"Mom, can we go get ice cream?" I begged. It was tradition to get ice cream after a recital or other performance—and tonight's performance was definitely one of my best.

"No, Wendy, it's late," Mom replied firmly.

"But Mom, please, oh pleeease?" I countered. "Please can we go get ice cream? We did so well tonight." Reluctantly, Mom agreed, and we stopped by Stan's Drive-In on the way to take Jackie home.

Jackie and I ate our ice cream in silence the rest of the way to Jackie's house. It was late, we were tired, and Mom was . . . something.

When we arrived back at our home, I hopped out of the VW and said hurriedly, "Thanks, Mom, for the ice cream." I ran downstairs to get in my pj's, brushing my teeth on the way to my basement bedroom. I loved my bedroom's Holly Hobbie wallpaper and bright orange shag carpet. Although it was in the basement, my bedroom was sunny. Mom hung the wallpaper all by herself late one night while I slept. She even finished off the room with a carefully hung Holly Hobbie art arrangement.

My bedroom was next to the storage room where our secret treats were sometimes hidden. Cary and I would sometimes sneak the treats out and hide the wrappers under our beds. Cary's bed was at the far end of the green shag playroom next to my bedroom door. Cary—along with his rats and hamsters and snakes—had to move to the basement when Annie was born. He didn't have his own bedroom yet, so he bunked in the playroom. I loved having him close, but I hated his rats.

Cary was already in bed when I skipped down the stairs and into my bedroom. After Mom put Annie in her crib, she came down the three flights of stairs and kissed Cary good night on her way to my room. She waited at my door while I said my bedtime prayers. She carefully tucked me in bed, pulling all the blankets tight around me, she kissed me good night—the same ritual she did every night. I quickly fell asleep.

That was the last time Mom ever touched me.

3

I Am Dead

The triumph of my play was just last night, but it seemed an eternity ago. My head was whirling. The room was spinning. *Will somebody please make it stop? Make the world stop turning so I can get off!* My life ended that day. I would be forever stuck at twelve.

How could I go on living when my mom, the woman who gave me life, was gone? How would I grow up and become a mom myself? How could I ever smile again when I felt like running away—but I couldn't because there was nowhere to run to? How could I think when the unthinkable had happened?

"Wendy, why don't you come and help me pick out some clothes for Annie?" Marjean said quietly. It took every ounce of energy I could summon to lift my body from the couch—my body felt like dying. No, it already felt dead.

Obediently, I walked back up the stairs with Marjean. We passed the closed bathroom door. I knew what lay behind it, and fear raced in my heart, but I methodically obeyed Marjean and led her into Annie's bedroom.

A ruffled, pale pink dress with white lace around the collar and matching bottoms was neatly laid out on the changing table—lovingly placed there by hands that would no longer pick up her baby to quiet her cries. Hands that had spent a lifetime in service to others. Hands that had wiped away tears and bandaged wounds that now lay lifeless behind a closed bathroom door.

"No!" I wanted to scream. "You can't be gone! Why? How? No!" I wanted to break down that door and burst into the bathroom to shake my mom awake. I wanted to save her. But instead, I gathered up Annie's clothes and carefully put them in the diaper bag while Marjean carried her down the stairs and placed her in the big brown buggy that was parked next to the piano in the living room. The buggy that Mom would never again push.

I quickly gathered up my own clothes, and the other children did too. With sleepy-bugs still in our eyes and still dressed in pajamas, we silently followed Marjean as she pushed Annie to her house down the street. Marjean was trying to protect us. She was letting us escape our house while Dad stayed there with the bishop to take care of whatever business you take care of when someone dies.

What do you do for five children when their mother dies? Marjean was not much older than our own mom, but she seemed to know exactly what to do—you let them be children.

It was Wednesday, April 16, and school was supposed to start in a few minutes, but Marjean let her three daughters stay home from school to play with us. After a breakfast of ice cream, the older children worked on putting together a big jigsaw puzzle—everyone, that is, except Cary. Cary sat in the same chair all day long, staring at the wall. He didn't talk, he didn't cry, and he didn't eat. He just stared straight ahead, stone-faced, without moving a muscle—frozen in time.

I played with Drew and Annie for a while and helped Ronette and Marjean do the dishes. Then Ronette and I escaped to her bedroom to talk and write. Ronette was one of my best friends. She and I used to play cowboys and Indians or Batman and Robin with our other neighborhood girlfriends before we graduated to seventh grade. Now we were more interested in boys, especially one in particular—Donny.

Donny was six years older than we were and was the heartthrob of the entire twelve-year old girls' church class taught by his mom, Kathy. Donny would take us in his blue beetle bug and do "swervy-dervies" in the church parking lot after it snowed. I wanted to marry Donny.

I was also mad at myself for not kissing him on a dare while he was sleeping. During one slumber party at Kathy's, four of us girls snuck into Donny's bedroom ever so quietly after he had gone to sleep. I bent down close to his face to kiss him, but I chickened out and pulled away several times. Finally, one of the other girls, exasperated at my multiple failed attempts, pushed me out of the way and said, "Oh brother! Just kiss him already!" and laid a big kiss right on his lips. The rest of the girls giggled and squealed and ran out of the room while Donny yelled at us. He was furious!

Ronette and I could talk about Donny for hours and hours. But today we didn't. We talked about heaven. Was my mom in heaven? I was certain she must be because she was perfect. Now all I needed to do was be perfect myself so I could see her again someday.

"Mom died of a heart attack," I explained. It was what I'd heard from my dad.

"I'm so sorry, Wendy," Ronette replied as we lay on her double bed. Bright sunshine streamed in through her south-facing window. Ronette was quite mature for a twelve-year-old. She talked to me about God's celestial heaven. Her dad was the bishop, and she seemed to know more than I did about heavenly things. I knew about Jesus and that he would come again someday, and I hoped I would see my mom again, but Ronette seemed to really know it in her heart.

I wished that I could be as certain as Ronette was. I felt wicked and imperfect, and I knew I would need to straighten out a lot of things if I was going to make it to heaven and see my mom. In Ronette's bedroom I wrote:

> *The time is coming closer to the coming of Christ our Redeemer. We must get prepared. When I look at myself and think about it, I really have got a lot of things I have to change about myself. I must change my ways!*

Oh how I wished I knew I would see her again! Oh how I wished she was still alive! It was all so unreal—I didn't feel alive. I was in my body, but I wasn't really.

I picked up my pencil again. I felt more alive while I was writing. The feel of my pencil on the paper brought me back to earth. My writing also revealed the weight I felt as a twelve-year-old girl—the weight of responsibility, of twelve-year-old sins, of loss, and of loneliness.

> *Every day counts. Live every hour as if it were your last; you never know. Don't ever go to bed or leave being mad at someone. You never know if that's the last time you're going to see them or not.*

4

She Didn't Die of a Heart Attack?

I woke up the next morning in my own bed in my Holly Hobbie bedroom. I felt numb and alone and afraid and grown-up and twelve all at the same time. I went upstairs to get Annie out of her crib and get her ready for the day. The bathroom door was open—and the bathroom was empty. Mom was still gone.

I felt hot tears come to my eyes, and I quickly pushed them away. I pushed them down into my heart, hidden where no one could see them. My lip quivered, so I bit it. My face turned to stone—or was it glass?—pretending to be big and strong. With Mom gone, I needed to take care of the kids and Dad—there was no room for tears.

"Wendy, someone is here to see you," Dad called from the living room. Kathy, my favorite teacher at church, had come to visit.

"Oh, Wendy," Kathy said as she embraced me in her arms. For an instant, I let myself feel Kathy's warmth. Then I pulled away and shyly looked down at the worn, olive-green living room carpet. "The girls in our class wanted to give you a special gift," Kathy said. She presented me with a beautiful white-dressed Madame Alexander collector's doll to add to the five I already had. Mom had started a Madame Alexander collection for me a few years earlier, and this doll, Scarlett, was a fitting tribute to Mom. She was an angel doll dressed in white, presented by an angel teacher whom I loved.

17

Kathy had beautiful, long, flowing auburn hair that reminded me of my mom's before she cut it off after Annie was born. Mom said short hair was easier to take care of with a little baby—that way Annie couldn't grab onto it and pull.

Kathy had a boat, and she took me and the other twelve-year-old girls waterskiing in the summertime. Kathy loved the water and the sunshine and the wind on her face. We loved baking in the sunshine with Kathy, even if we were blistered and peeling red when we went home.

Kathy gave great boyfriend advice. Her two daughters, Lisa and Laurie, were both cheerleaders in high school, and their older brother, Donny, was a star basketball player. As twelve-year-olds, we looked up to these two girls, who seemed to us to have lots of boyfriends. Kathy, for her part, would try to protect us from the boys she didn't think were good enough for us. She taught us to keep high standards so we could some day be married in our church's temple.

You could only go to the temple if you lived the way God wanted his daughters to live—if you were morally clean in every way. You had to dress modestly and not have sex or anything close to sex before you got married. Kathy warned us to stay away from boys who would try to take advantage of us and repeated the strict commandment from our church to not date before we were sixteen.

Kathy was forever young. She had a ready smile and welcomed us into her life. She loved us no matter what our backgrounds—rich or poor, skinny or fat, smart or pretty or not. It didn't matter to Kathy; she instantly made us feel like part of her family. Her home was a favorite hangout place for me and my girlfriends.

"Wendy, let's go shopping for a dress for the funeral," said Kathy. I didn't say much, but I put on my shoes and jacket and climbed into Kathy's truck. It was good to get out of the house, which was crowded with aunts and uncles and neighbors—a steady stream of people who came to help Dad with funeral arrangements, drop off a card or goodies or flowers, or help take care of the kids. It was overflowing with people—everyone except Mom.

Kathy rescued me from that madness and took me to a little shop downtown. The shop was filled with clothes racks stuffed with long dresses, short dresses, skirts, and blouses—lifeless forms that hung from the racks like they were dead too. I wanted to hide between the racks and disappear, smothered by these ghosts.

"Here are some beautiful dresses," Kathy said as she led me to one of the crowded racks. "Why don't you try one on?" She handed me a long, flowing, beige Gunne Sax dress that was cut low, laced up the front, and had big, sheer, puffy long sleeves. It looked like a dress someone would wear to their senior prom in high school.

"Not quite right," Kathy said when I tried it on for her. I quickly changed back into my jeans and T-shirt. We looked through some more long dresses, and Kathy pulled out a simple white empire-waist short-sleeved dress with a pink satin tie in the back—perfect for a twelve-year-old.

I tried it on and looked at myself in the mirror. For the first time since Mom died the day before, something felt right. White. Pure. Heavenly. The color of angels. I would match my mom's white burial dress. Perfect. White.

I was silent on the ride home, thinking about the viewing the next day. Hot tears surfaced again, but I forced them back and swallowed hard, covering them with stone.

"Thank you, Kathy. The dress is really pretty," I said as she dropped me off at home. I carefully carried the dress to my bedroom and lovingly hung it in my closet. It reminded me of the dress I'd worn when I was baptized into our church at age eight. I felt clean and pure after being buried in the water and having the Holy Ghost confirmed on me by hands laid on my head. I felt perfectly clean, all my sins washed away. I wanted to stay perfect forever.

Now I felt heavy and old and stained with sadness. But I would wear white tomorrow in my mom's memory, for she was perfect.

The house was still busy with adults, so I went with the other kids back to Marjean's home to finish the puzzle we had started the day before. While we worked on the puzzle, Annie fell asleep in her buggy. Drew lay down on the couch for a nap, so while Marie played upstairs with Marci, Ronette and I went outside to play kick the can with our neighborhood friends, including Brad and Brad.

I ran and hid and laughed and joked with my friends, and it felt for a moment like life could be normal again—until cute Brad, the police chief's son, interrupted the fantasy. "I know how your mom died," he said.

"She died of a heart attack," I replied.

"No she didn't. She shot herself," Brad countered.

"No, she had a heart attack!" I said angrily, shocked at what I had just heard. My head tingled. I forced myself to stay standing, afraid I might pass out.

Brad said authoritatively, "My dad is the chief of police and went to investigate, and he told me your mom shot herself in the bathroom."

"No she didn't!" I yelled back. I ran up the street, panic building in my heart. The world closed in around me. Darkness encircled me. I couldn't breathe. My hands were sweating. My ears were deaf. I ran for my life. My legs were shaking, barely able to hold me up as I threw open the front door.

"Dad!" I gasped, out of breath and out of life. "Brad said Mom shot herself!" I yelled hysterically. "But she died of a heart attack, didn't she?!" I felt out of control. Terrorized. I looked for any reassurance that my story—the story Dad had told me and my younger siblings— was right. "Didn't she?!" I yelled again.

My dad looked stunned. My mom's oldest sister, Aunt Carol, who sitting on the couch next to Dad, said quietly, "You'd better go talk to her."

I ran down the stairs to my bedroom and slammed my bedroom door. I fell on my bed, buried my face in my pillow, and sobbed and sobbed. I couldn't contain the tears any longer. How could it be? It couldn't be! She couldn't! She didn't! How could she? How could anyone shoot themselves? Oh, God, why? Where are you? Where is she? Darkness thickened around me.

Dad came in quietly and sat gingerly at the foot of my bed. It was awkward for him to be in my bedroom. I don't think he had ever come in there except to fix the furnace or to go to the storage room where the guns were kept. Now he sat next to me, still and distant.

"Yes, Wendy. Mom shot herself," I heard Dad say from what seemed to be miles away. Although I felt like kicking and screaming, I watched myself lay on my bed in disbelief as though I were two separate people. Dad didn't say much. He didn't know how. And then he left me. Alone. Alone in my bedroom. My haunted bedroom.

Afraid.

5

Rocks

John, I don't want to be angry anymore," I told my therapist. My youngest son, nearly twenty-year-old William, had just returned home sixteen months early from a two-year mission for our church because he was found by our church leaders to be unworthy to serve. He hadn't confessed or repented of certain sins prior to his mission, and now he had to go through a strict repentance process for six to twelve months before he could go back.

I was livid at the requirements thrust upon William by these men who I thought were rigid and archaic in their interpretation of Christ's law. I wasn't even certain I believed in Jesus Christ anymore, and I hated seeing my son in pain. If there was a Christ, I thought, surely he would not approve of this public display of retribution for my son's sins.

I was concerned for William not simply because I was his mom and he was my youngest of four children but also because William had suffered a major depressive episode three years earlier. We had nearly lost him.

My husband, Mark, and I had returned home early from a class one evening to find William lying in the fetal position on the couch, unable to move. He had just begun a suicide attempt. He planned to take all of the pills in the cupboard. An angel friend's phone call had interrupted that attempt just as William took the first pills—herbs he hoped would calm him before he moved on to the rest of the prescription drugs he had carefully lined up on the counter.

I had already lived through one suicide and nearly weathered another. Mark had gone through some dark days after he had been diagnosed with multiple sclerosis. One day, I came home from work to a voicemail message from Mark saying good-bye to me and the kids. The police put out an APB, and I gathered my children around me. The bishop came over, and we knelt in family prayer, begging for a miracle—an all-too-familiar scene that took me back to the day when I was twelve and another bishop knelt with a young family.

We got our miracle when Mark phoned from the hospital and told me he was being admitted to the psychiatric ward, where he began the slow recovery from his painful depression. Mark lived. Mom died.

Finding William so close to death sent me back to those dark days. I couldn't do it again. The thought of losing my youngest son to suicide was almost more than I could bear. I knew I couldn't live if he died that way. My heart would break.

Through the grace of God, William's own determination, and the intervention of earthly and heavenly angels, William had recovered and moved forward, excelling in high school. He won several regional and state awards in cross-country, track, vocal performance, musical theater, and creative writing. We kept busy attending all of William's extracurricular activities, and despite his busy schedule, William graduated from high school with honors. He even got to sing the national anthem at the graduation ceremony with four of his choir buddies. He went on to complete a summer term at Brigham Young University before leaving for his much-anticipated mission.

Now he was home, sad, and heavy—and burdened with thoughts of failure. And I hurt for him. My heart hurt.

I cried and I screamed—but not in front of William. I didn't want him to sense my anger. I didn't want my own rage to stand in the way of William's decision to go back on his mission, no matter what the cost or penalty. He was determined to do whatever was required of him, and he asked us to shake him out of it if we saw him slip into another depression.

Despite the love and support we felt from our congregation, I hurt for William. And I was mad. I wanted to give our church leaders a piece of my mind—to advocate on William's behalf. But I was helpless to change the outcome. So instead of yelling at the church leaders or yelling at God, I decided I might need professional help to rid myself of the anger that simmered just below the surface and every now and then boiled over with words I inevitably regretted. I wanted to change.

"How many visits do you think I'll need?" I asked my therapist, John.

"Oh, we should be done in four or five visits," he replied as he showed me a strategy for breaking the anger cycle.

I tried really hard for the month before the next visit to break that cycle. I tried to be perfect. William progressed on his road to repentance. He returned to the mission where he'd been serving and the people he loved so much, fulfilling a complete and honorable mission. And I journaled all of my angry thoughts, analyzing each feeling and trying to change. I was somewhat successful at controlling my words, but I couldn't rid myself of the rage. It took nearly every ounce of energy I had to push the feeling down my throat and smile instead of scream.

I had laid rocks in my heart one by one over the years, and they were heavy. I felt like two people—the person I should be outside looking in at the person I really was—the screaming maniac with a big smile pretending to be happy, who every now and then would blow up and say something she later regretted.

Right now I needed to feel love and patience, but I couldn't. I didn't know how to feel. I didn't know how to love. I felt only anger—or nothing.

I tried to strip away my anger over the next two months. I discovered that underneath all that rage, under the rocks carefully placed over the years, was deep sadness—that's all. Deep sorrow and loneliness buried in my heart.

No one would have guessed the pain I felt—pain that occasionally escaped as tears when alone in the bathroom with the water running so no one could hear. Pain that was masked as anger.

People would tell me that I was a strong woman—a successful nurse manager, an MBA graduate at the top of the class, a goal-directed, action-oriented, self-motivated, driven woman. I was the sole provider for our family. I returned to nursing school with three little children when Mark was diagnosed with multiple sclerosis six years into our marriage. William was born after my second year of school, and I didn't miss a beat, returning to class the week after I delivered him.

I was strong, I had a ready smile, and I could overcome any

challenge. I'd learned how to when I was twelve. But I couldn't get rid of the anger.

On my fourth visit—the visit where I was supposed to be cured—I said, "John, I think I need to process my mother's death. She committed suicide when I was twelve, and I never had any therapy." I was terrified to start this journey, but while trying to strip away anger, I had peeked under the pile of rocks. All I saw was a hole—a deep, lonely, sad emptiness buried so many years ago.

And that terrified me even more.

6

Mom Wanted Heaven

APRIL 18, 1975

I lay on my bed, unable to move and wrapped in my yellow-and-white plaid quilt, which was tied with bright orange yarn to match my carpet. I made the quilt in 4-H with my church girlfriends, and it had won a red ribbon in the County Fair just the month before. Mom had carefully finished the edges with white eyelet lace, but now she was gone. Forever.

I breathed heavily, and my eyes darted from the furnace door on the left of my bed to the storage room door at its foot. My mom and my cousin Karen had said they'd seen a ghost there in the middle of the day. Karen used to babysit us, and she described the ghost as a man in the storage room where the guns were kept. Karen said he came after Mom and Karen not long before Mom shot herself. Karen and Mom ran up the stairs, seeking safety from the frightening visitation—the evil that sought Mom's destruction.

Now the ghosts were after me. I was afraid that someone might be hiding in the storage room, waiting for my dad to leave so the murderer could come out and kill me too. I jumped when the furnace turned on. Was the killer in the furnace room? Even though the heat duct was on the ceiling just above my head, I couldn't get warm. I shivered uncontrollably. Death by suicide felt cold and dark and evil, and my brain couldn't stop spinning.

I lay in my bed, waiting for my would-be attacker until it was dark outside my small basement window. My muscles were taut, my heart pounded, and my head hurt. I didn't kneel by my bed to say my prayers for fear that my assailant would attack me when my eyes were closed. I hoped my quilt would protect me.

Finally, sleep overcame me, and I closed my eyes, my quilt still wrapped tightly around me up to my chin. I don't know how long I slept that night before ghosts invaded my dreams— my mother's ghost and ghosts of murderers chasing me to kill me too. I awoke with a start, my heart racing, my hands clenched, my quilt wet with sweat. I didn't have my glasses on, but I knew there were ghosts in the shadows. I could see them moving in the darkness.

Who would save me now? "Dad!" I screamed as loud as I could. "Help! Help me! Dad!!" I yelled and yelled, but he couldn't hear me three floors up. "Dad!!" I screamed again. Finally, I shot out of bed and ran up the stairs as fast as I could to the protection of my mom and dad's bedroom—only Mom wasn't there.

Dad let me lie down on the bed in Mom's spot, and I curled up, facing the closet where her clothes still hung. My silent tears wet her pillow, and I wished she could kiss me good night just one more time.

Morning finally came, but sleep did not. I climbed out of bed and went into the bathroom—the bathroom at the top of the stairs where Mom had shot herself just two days earlier. I shuddered, thinking of the grizzly deed, and imagined Mom lying on the floor in a big pool of sticky blood. I couldn't see any evidence that she had killed herself just two mornings ago in that very bathroom. The knickknacks and the fancy soap in the gold soap dish that Mom had carefully placed on the countertops were untouched. Even her eyelash curler and the comb she used to comb her eyebrows were still on the shelf below the big mirror above the sink—everything placed exactly like it was three days earlier.

I pushed aside thoughts of Mom's death and the ghosts that haunted me, and I hurried to get ready for school. Life must go on, after all. Like I wrote in my diary the day Mom died:

> Life is made up of the little things that happen, not the big things. The smiles, the first time a baby walks or talks, the love little children have for one another.

I ran down the stairs to join my dad and my siblings for scripture reading and family prayer before heading off to school. Just before

Ronette's dad rang the doorbell to pick me up, we read this verse in our church's scriptures:

I will go and do the things which the Lord hath commanded, for I know that the Lord giveth no commandments unto the children of men, save he shall prepare a way for them that they may accomplish the thing which he commandeth them. (1 Nephi 3:7)

Since the Lord had allowed my mom to die by suicide, I knew I could do whatever was required of me, no matter how hard it was—at least, that's what the scripture said to me: this was hard, but I could do it. I was late for school, and the world hadn't stopped turning to let me off, so I had to say good-bye to Dad and Annie and Cary and Drew and Marie and go face seventh grade again with my good friend Ronette.

At school, I knew everyone was whispering about me, but I put on my armor—my glass face and my stone heart—and I smiled and tried to fit in. In fourth period English, I laughed with my friends who'd put chalk on Mr. Bennett's chair as we waited for him to sit down. "Ruff, ruff," said the girl who sat behind me. She had flipped her long hair up over her face, put her hoodie on her head, and crawled up to peer over Mr. Bennett's desk while he was writing on the chalk board. At the same time, several other students crawled out the window to escape his class. Mr. Bennett tried to ignore the girl and kept writing with his back turned. "Ruff, ruff!" she said again. This time, Mr. Bennett turned around, his face red and his nostrils flaring. Mr. Bennett had the biggest nose I had ever seen. I could look straight up it from my front row desk and see all the crusties that were stuck there—an awful sight that could turn your stomach. This time, though, I couldn't help but laugh. And Mr. Bennett was mad. He had lost control of the class completely.

"Wendy, please read from page 106," Mr. Bennett said. We were reading Old Yeller, and I wasn't the least bit interested in the book.

"I don't know how to read," I said sarcastically, looking around to make sure I was cool with my friends. This made Mr. Bennett even madder.

He asked me to come out into the hall with him. "Wendy," he said sternly, "I know your mom just died, and I'm going to give you an A, but I need you to be respectful and try to do the work."

I wasn't sure why I was called out into the hall while everyone else was escaping the class through the window, but I was embarrassed and somewhat ashamed at my behavior. But instead of apologizing, I bragged after school that I was going to get an A in the class. Within myself, though, I knew I didn't deserve it.

The rest of school that day was a blur. I watched myself laugh and joke with my friends, but on the inside I was crying and afraid and alone. I was different. I looked around and didn't see anyone without a mom. I knew of one kid whose mom had cancer, but she was still alive. My mom was dead. She'd shot herself—a secret I would protect for years.

After school, I opened the front door of our house and half expected to see Mom there, sitting in the kitchen on her green-and-blue plaid chair with her legs swinging over the armrest that had been shredded by our Siamese cat, Blue. She should have been on the phone with one of her sisters.

I remembered one of her conversations from just a week or two ago. "Grace, I'm not afraid to die. I know where I'm going, and it's beautiful there," she'd said to her sister on the other end of the phone. After a long pause, she emphatically repeated, "I'm not afraid to die."

Mom had "died" six months earlier when she'd had a cardiac arrest. She left her body and flew to her mountain home. I must have told some of my classmates, because the week after her near-death experience, someone handed me a note in class. When I opened it, I found a rendition of an ugly, pimpled Wendy with the words "Dead Mommy" scribbled on top of the page.

I ran home to Mom and crawled on her bed next to her. She was too weak to move, but she tried to comfort me with words when I showed her the crumpled note.

"Mom, look at what they said!" I cried.

"Wendy, I know it's not very nice, but they just don't understand," Mom said quietly. She seemed distant. She gazed toward heaven, her head motionless on her pillow.

She then recounted the experience she'd had when her heart had stopped for several minutes. She found herself outside of her body, free from the pain of her crushing chest and aching scars—reminders of when she had been engulfed in flames at three years old. Her dress had caught on fire from a cupcake candle, and when she ran to her dad, the breeze fanned the flames. Her dad snatched her in his arms and rolled with her on the ground, extinguishing the flames, but her skin was charred all over her back and down her arm—third-degree burns that required painful dressing changes each day. The burnt skin stuck to the bandages, and Mom cried out in pain when the doctor tried to remove them. They peeled off with a blackened sheet of flesh.

Mom's dad, Grandpa Rowley, had died five years earlier, right before Father's Day 1969. The Father's Day letter Mom wrote to him thanking him for saving her life arrived too late. But now that she'd left her body, she could thank him in person. And she could see her mom, Grandma Eva, who had died when Mom was seventeen. Mom was free at last and on her way to heaven.

But first, one last stop at her mountain retreat. Out of her body, Mom saw green grass covered with wildflowers at the water's edge. Marie was there, but she was all grown up. She was even taller than Mom—an angel daughter with long blonde hair falling down her back. Marie comforted her. "Mom, everything is going to be okay," Marie said gently. Mom knew then that she wasn't going to see her children raised, but she was overcome with peace and love. Everything was going to be okay. Her pain had been swallowed up in the light of heaven. She was free.

Just as Mom was about to leave this heaven on earth, she heard Dad command her spirit to return to her body. Under the date October 1, 1974, Dad described in his memoir:

She was fading fast and lapsing into a coma. You could see the concerned faces on each of us. We didn't want her to die. Dr. Stan made her a concoction of licorice root and some other stimulant herbs, but it was too late. Stan said, "I think she is gone." I was in near panic as I replied, "Do you have some oil?" I wanted to give her a blessing. It seemed like an eternity before Stan came back into the room with the oil. My dad anointed her head, and I pronounced the blessing. No sooner had the three of us priesthood bearers removed our hands from her head than Linda started to respond and come out of her unconscious state.

In his journal, Dad wrote, "Through an exercise of faith and the power of the priesthood, the Lord has preserved her life thus far."

Mom found herself back in her crushed, weakened body—to face life a little longer. She was never quite the same after that. Her smile must have stayed in heaven. And as hard as she tried, she couldn't regain her strength. She was haunted by spirits—evil spirits bent on leading her to hell. But she wanted heaven. And she shot herself to get there.

7

Dressed in White

I was in a daze when I got home from school on Friday, going through the motions of life on the second day after Mom shot herself. *Did I get homework today? I don't know. Did it really matter if I did? No. Life is made up of the little things.*

Adults were everywhere—aunts and uncles, Grandma and Grandpa, neighbors, friends, church members—people who supported my dad through this dark time. People summoned to help take care of my little brothers and sisters. It was suffocating. And I felt so alone.

I didn't dare go downstairs by myself, so I went upstairs to Mom's bedroom. She wasn't there. I looked in the other bedrooms. Not there either. Everywhere I looked reminded me of Mom, but she was still gone. God, please bring her back, I pleaded. I will be good. I will be perfect. This couldn't be happening. It didn't feel real.

I walked past the bathroom and looked for any signs of the recent murder. Nothing. Everything was scoured—the secret hidden away where no one could find it.

I escaped the demons by going to Kathy's home with Ronette for a few hours. Kathy's home felt warm and light and inviting—like heaven compared to the cold, haunted hell of my house. My empty house without my mom—my murdered mom. Murdered by her own hand.

Ronette and I sat on the couch with Kathy, and she laughed with us as I recounted the experience in Mr. Bennett's classroom. "Oh dear." She smiled. "You kids better treat him a little nicer."

"I know, but he's just such a weirdo," I said. Although Ronette wasn't in that class, she agreed that he wasn't a very good teacher.

Kathy made us root beer floats, and we hurried to sip down the root beer before it bubbled over the side of the glass. Just as we finished the floats, Donny came roaring home in his blue beetle. My heart skipped a beat as he bounded through the front door.

"Hi Mom—oh, and hi Wendy and Ronette," he said as he threw his books on the floor. He picked up his guitar, which was leaning against the far corner of the room, and plopped down cross-legged in the center of the braided rug right in front of the couch we were sitting on.

"Do you guys want to hear a song I just wrote?" We nodded yes, too shy to say anything to a boy six years older than we were—the boy I hoped to someday marry.

Donny plucked the strings with ease and sang about finding lost love. I imagined he was singing about me, and I dreamt of holding hands and running barefoot through meadows with my summertime dress billowing out behind me. It was all so romantic—me and Ronette sitting on the couch with our knees to our chests, listening to Donny sing and play the guitar.

Before I knew it, it was time to get ready for the viewing. "Goodbye, Kathy. I'll see you tonight," I said as Ronette and I ran home.

"Wendy, you need to hustle. We need to leave in thirty minutes," Dad said anxiously as I hurried downstairs to change into my angel-white dress.

Cary sat on his bed at the far end of the playroom, already in his Sunday clothes. He protected me from ghosts while I changed clothes in my haunted bedroom.

Dad said it was time to leave. "Cary, we'd better hurry," I said, coaxing him upstairs.

At the funeral home, I was brave and strong and numb, greeting hundreds of people I didn't know in a line that went on for miles. I stood next to Dad beside mom's casket and shook hands and hugged people I'd never seen before. My best friends from first grade, Karen and Colleen, came to see Mom. We'd moved from their neighborhood before second grade, and I hadn't seen them for a year or two. It was good to see their familiar faces. Their parents hugged me and said the line for the viewing wrapped around the building twice. I groaned inside because my feet were tired and I didn't want to hug one more stranger.

I was relieved when my girlfriends from church came through with their parents and coaxed my dad into letting me leave early with them to go to Arlene's sleepover birthday party. Cary, Marie, and Drew had left with one of the many adult volunteers as soon as the viewing started, and Annie was at home with a babysitter, but I had accompanied my dad in line for what seemed to be hours. Now I was free—for the night, anyway.

Arlene's dad had built their house by himself many years before. It had the steepest, narrowest staircase that I had ever seen outside of pioneer homes. I would always hold on for dear life when coming down those stairs from their sewing room. Except for the handrail, it felt like I was coming down a ladder facing forward. One misstep and you would break your neck. It had a haunted house look, and some people said they saw ghosts in the upstairs windows, but tonight it didn't feel haunted to me.

Arlene's mom, Helen, volunteered as our 4-H leader, and all my church girlfriends participated in her 4-H club. Helen taught us to sew, ski, bake, draw, and do genealogy. She had traced several of her own ancestors all the way back to Adam and Eve.

Helen would take us to the genealogy library and teach us how to do our own research. I turned the microfilm wheel as fast as I could to scan through the stacks of old birth certificates, death certificates, and journal entries. It was a treasure hunt that linked me to both kings and paupers as far back as 1400 AD. I felt bigger and more important when I read the accounts of ancestors who fought in the revolutionary war or pioneers who crossed the plains in handcarts. I sometimes wished I lived in a log cabin and read by candlelight and farmed the land in God's open expanse of earth. But I resigned myself to reading about my ancestors who did.

I was proud of my association with those distant relatives. I even won a blue ribbon at the County Fair for my book of remembrance genealogy thanks to Mom's final touches. She let me raid her own book of remembrance for some of the stories of our great- and great-great-grandparents. Now she was in heaven with those same grandparents—or was she? I couldn't be sure. Where do you go when you shoot yourself?

I set aside thoughts of death, guns, and ghosts and tried to fit in with my friends. "I get the front seat," Cindy called as the rest of us scrambled into the familiar van that hauled six or seven girls each week to our various 4-H activities and Saturday ski lessons. Ronette and I sat in the back while we headed to the late-night showing of *Escape to Witch Mountain*.

❧ ❧

"Wendy, wake up." Arlene shook me. "The show is over." I had just closed my eyes for a minute, but now I could hardly move. We left the theater and headed to Arlene's. Once there, I curled up on the living room floor with my pillow and my quilt and immediately fell asleep. I was exhausted. I slept straight through cake and ice cream and late-night television clear to breakfast. I felt safe in the company of my friends, and ghosts didn't haunt my dreams.

"Wendy, we'd better get you home," Helen said after breakfast. "You need to get ready for the funeral."

I reluctantly said good-bye to the girls and climbed into the front seat of the van, still in my pajamas, with my pillow and blanket in my lap. Just three days before, I had followed another friend's mom to her house in my pajamas, and now Arlene's mom was taking me home—again in my pajamas. All of these moms—but none of them were mine.

8

Buried Alive

Dad, is that where Mom shot herself?" I asked, pointing to a diagonal, fleshy, moist open slit on one side of her neck. It peeked out behind her white angel dress, which matched my own white dress.

I had barely glanced at Mom the night before, but now I looked. And what I saw haunted me for years. My dead mom—only she didn't look like my mom. Someone had curled her short hair and caked makeup on her perfect face.

Mom was a no-frills kind of girl whose preferred wardrobe consisted of 501 Levi jeans and a T-shirt. In earlier years, she'd worn her hair long, curling it for special occasions. But mostly she pulled it back in a ponytail. And she didn't wear much makeup—she didn't need to. Her blemish-free olive skin had a natural glow that accentuated her high cheekbones. She was stunningly beautiful.

But this morning she looked dead—a cold wax figure with lipstick and short hair. All made up to go to heaven—or was it hell?

I studied Mom's face. If I looked long enough, maybe she would open her eyes and start breathing again. But then again, she might grab me like in a horror show. I summoned all my courage and touched the weathered fingers clasped below her waist. I withdrew quickly. She was so cold and stiff and heavy—dead.

The slit in her throat looked ghastly, oozing, and raw. "That is where they drained all the blood out of her so they could embalm her,"

Dad explained as he pulled Mom's ruffled collar over her neck. "She shot herself in her stomach," he said, placing his hand on his own.

My brain was jumbled again, trying to make sense of all the horror. *They slit her throat to drain her blood? How much blood was in the bathroom? How much blood did they have to drain? Did she suffer? Did she die instantly? Why? How? Maybe she didn't mean to. Maybe it was an accident. Maybe she was murdered. Maybe she was possessed. No!*

I wanted to scream. But instead I stared at Mom as Dad continued, "She leaned over the rifle and shot herself in the stomach. The bullet went out the ceiling."

I imagined her lying in a pool of blood with the gun next to her. She would still be in her pajamas too. *Oh, God, please bring her back to me!* I shouted in my mind while I stared at her beautiful, still, heavy, cold, lifeless body.

The room was filled to overflowing with flowers gifted in Mom's memory—red roses, pink carnations, white daisies—all of Mom's favorites. They represented her life, cut short like blossoms cut from the bush. The rose heart wreath labeled *Mom* stood at the head of the casket as if to remind the world that she was my mom. And that she was no more.

I was unaware that the extended family had all gathered in the room where Mom still lay in her casket. Dad had spared no expense on Mom's funeral arrangements. He chose the finest casket money could buy, and he purchased new burial clothes—a heavenly white dress normally worn in our church's temple, where those worthy are married and where they learn how to return back to heaven when they die. Dad even purchased twelve burial plots just in case—one for him and Mom, plus ten more for children or grandparents who might need them when their time on Earth came to an end.

There was standing room only in this already crowded room as Mom's eight older and Dad's six younger siblings, Grandma and Grandpa, the bishop, and countless cousins, aunts, and uncles filtered in. I stood at the front next to the casket with Dad. The bishop asked us all to join in a family prayer led by Grandpa, Dad's dad. I didn't want to close my eyes, which were fixed on Mom, but I obediently bowed my head and tried to keep from crying as Grandpa pled for comfort from God. He asked God to give us understanding. But how can anyone ever understand? Can God grant understanding of the incomprehensible?

Grandpa asked for a blessing on each of the children. "Wendy, Cary, Marie, Drew, and Annie all carry with them a piece of her life and her love," he said. I wished that was true. But more important, I wished that she was still alive—that she could be returned to us.

At the conclusion of the prayer, I opened my eyes and wiped away the tears I had tried to suppress. And I looked again at Mom—I longed for her to take one more breath.

"Wendy, do you want to give her a kiss before they close the casket?" one man asked. I shuddered at the thought and shook my head no. I couldn't kiss her cold, dead flesh. But I couldn't stop staring. I bit my lip as they opened the bottom half of the casket so we could see her whole body one last time. I went up and touched her hand again—still dead. I felt out of body too—as cold as Mom. Dead.

And then they closed the casket. I couldn't breathe. My head was whirling. The room was spinning. I couldn't see her. I couldn't touch her. I wouldn't feel her ever again. She was gone forever. And I couldn't keep back the tears.

No! I wanted to shout. *God, don't take her away from us!*

I wanted to throw my body on top of Mom's and fight with all my power and might to prevent that door from closing. I wanted to save Mom from the darkness—to rescue her from death and keep her with me. *She can't go,* I cried from deep within myself. *I still need her! No!*

A piece of my soul left my body and followed Mom into the darkness—that deep abyss—and lay down next to Mom to be buried with her. The closed casket was suffocating, but try as I might, I couldn't claw my way out. I couldn't open the door. I couldn't see the light. I was dead.

9

My Broken Heart

John, my heart hurts," I said, clutching my chest. "I think I'm going to have a heart attack!" I couldn't catch my breath, my eyes couldn't focus, and my hands were sweaty but my body was ice cold as I recounted memories from my twelve-year-old childhood. Memories of death and blood and darkness—eternal darkness. I was dark.

I had buried these memories and tried to bury the pain with cold earth—stones on top of a closed casket. After all the anger, all I'd uncovered was sadness. My heart hurt.

John didn't try to rescue me from certain death—he didn't try to intervene to take away the pain or perform CPR. He merely listened as I shared bits and pieces of a long-ago life—details I had never shared with anyone. I couldn't.

Instead, I'd worn a glass face—a mask painted with my mom's smile. I'd tried to fit in. In thirty-six years I had never met anyone else whose mother had killed herself when they were a kid. But maybe they were just silent too.

"She died of a heart attack," I'd told a friend after my second baby, Jordan, was born—a line I had rehearsed for many years. It was bad enough not having a mom to hold her two grandbabies, let alone having to endure the judgment and the gossip and the questions—and the pain—that would surely follow a confession of her true cause of death.

"Gunshot wound" is all that was mentioned on the death certificate,

39

which was carefully hidden away—a well-orchestrated cover-up to protect the children and unborn grandchildren of a thirty-one-year-old mom who shot herself.

"How did Grandma die?" my oldest son, nineteen-year-old Aaron, asked while filling out his church mission application. He knew she'd died when I was young, but the application asked for cause of death.

I was silent. My heart raced with adrenaline accompanied by fear. I felt like running away. I nervously looked at my husband and back at my son. Before we were married, I had shared with Mark how my mom died, but I had successfully hidden the truth from my four children for nineteen years. I rarely talked about my mom except to share how perfect she was. We put Angie the Angel—the angel Mom got from her mom and that Dad passed on to me—on top of our Christmas tree every year, but that was as close as I got. I didn't even have a picture of Mom in our home. My children didn't know her, and they didn't know me—at least, not this part of me I'd buried so long ago.

"Suicide—she shot herself," I heard myself say. And now Aaron was silent. I went on to say what I had rehearsed several times in my mind and what I had shared with the few people who knew about Mom's death: "She was really sick. She had a cardiac arrest six months before, and she never got better." I tried to explain the unexplainable.

I told Aaron about the high-ranking church official my dad was privileged to escort a few days after Mom's death. Dad was in our church priesthood leadership—a counselor to the bishop. As Dad described, Ezra Taft Benson—the president of our church's twelve apostles at the time—looked into the heavens and declared, "Your wife did not pull the trigger, and if you live worthily, you will be in the celestial kingdom with her." The celestial kingdom, the highest mansion in heaven prepared for my dad and mom—if he was worthy.

Surely I would see Mom again. That promise had to be real. But I felt nothing even as I described this sacred event—this divine revelation given to my dad by a holy man of God. I felt empty and distant.

Mark called the rest of the children into the living room with Aaron so I could share with them the rehearsed description of how and why my mom died. "She was sick. She was sad. It was hard. She didn't pull the trigger."

All the children looked silently at the floor, unsure of what to say or how to feel. I had tried to protect them, fearing that if they knew how their grandma died they might consider suicide as a way out of pain, and I couldn't bear to lose them. Or maybe I just couldn't bear my own pain—pain hidden under layers of cold earth.

Fifteen-year-old Becca broke the silence and confessed, "I found her death certificate when I was nine and was confused by why it said 'gunshot wound' as the cause of death." She said she'd asked about it, but I had no memory of that conversation. She had never dared talk about it again. Seventeen-year-old Jordan had known for years—as long as he could remember. He had overheard a relative talking about it many years before but had kept the secret to himself. I never knew my children carried unanswered questions for all these years—unanswered questions and unspoken, silent, buried fear.

As quickly as I shared with my children how Mom had died, I replaced the stones, covered the fear, and hid the tears—and then cried alone in the bathroom with the water running.

My therapist, John, looked at me as I tried to describe the pieces of that terrible day—the bathroom, the gun, my mom. Eventually his training provided what were probably meant to be comforting words: "That must have been hard."

Hard? I thought. *You have no idea! I feel dead!*

In a desperate attempt to help John understand a measure of the pain I felt, I read to him from my journal entry of January 19, 2011:

> *If I could cry enough tears to take away the pain, I'm sure the seas couldn't contain them all. When mom leaned over the gun, as dad described, in her pink nightgown, and pulled the trigger, the bullet pierced through her stomach and out the roof. At that very moment, the same bullet pierced my heart and left a gaping hole. A void that has never been filled and never will be filled. Mom shot each of her children when she shot herself—and a piece of us died with her.*

And John was silent.

10

The Valley of Death

Tears ran down my cheeks as I took my place next to Dad behind the closed casket that carried my dead mom. Dad wrapped his arm around me to steady me. I could hardly keep from falling. My siblings, Annie in my grandpa's arms, followed us as we walked solemnly down the chapel aisle.

More than one thousand people stood in humble reverence, watching as we took our places on the front bench—an arm's reach away from Mom's casket in front of us. Even the gym and stage at the back of the chapel were filled to capacity. Friends, family, business associates, and church members attended to offer support to a grieving husband and his desolate children.

The bishop stood at the pulpit and said, "Brothers and sisters, friends and family members, we unite at this solemn occasion and pay tribute to the life of Linda."

I tried to be brave as I sat next to Dad, but my tears ran freely. *Where is Mom?* I thought. *Is she here? Can she see how much I miss her? Can she see how much I love her?*

If only God could grant me one last glimpse—not of her dead body, but of her living, breathing, vibrant soul, of her smile, her sunshine, her love.

Where is she? I thought again. The bishop spoke of her goodness— her selfless service of reaching out to those who hurt and helping heal the sick and brokenhearted. "We can't judge," he said. Surely she must be in heaven.

He read the words Mom had penned just six months earlier, shortly after her heart failed. Mom had written to her children about a loving Heavenly Father who desires us to return to him. "We must always be mindful of our great responsibility to ourselves and to our Heavenly Father," she wrote. "To act our very best and do our very best, whatever it may be, so that we can return again to live with Him—because He loves us so very, very much and *longs* for our return when our mission and trials in this life are over."

And her trials in this life were over—but what about the next? Would God accept her into his arms with her own blood on her hands? Would Jesus Christ redeem her and remove her stain with the blood of his atonement so she could progress to the eternal life of which she spoke?

The only thing my brain could comprehend was that Mom was gone—her lifeless body enclosed in a dark, silent casket. I stared at the casket and cried.

Someone sang "I Am a Child of God," and I cried. *I am a child—a twelve-year-old child!* She continued singing: "Has given me an earthly home, with parents kind and dear."

But what about my *earthly home? Where are my parents kind and dear? My mom is gone from this earth. She is dead. I am alone. And lost. And afraid. And sad.*

I stared at the casket through tears for the rest of the meeting. Alone in a sea of people—just me and Mom. I didn't hear the words that were spoken, but I thought of heaven, and I tried to believe in it. I tried to believe that God loved me and that he loved my mom. I tried to believe that there really were angels. I tried to believe that I could go on. With God's help I could do anything, right?

Mom's good friend Larry tried to sing "O My Father." He sobbed. The words wouldn't come.

He started again. His deep voice resonated in my heart, and I felt God's arms around me, comforting my soul as he sang:

> *In the heavens are parents single?*
> *No, the thought makes reason stare!*
> *Truth is reason; truth eternal*
> *Tells me I've a mother there.*

God reached down and touched my heart, and I longed to return to Him in my heavenly home. I knew for that brief moment that Mom—my mom—was in heaven. And I missed her. And I knew that I had to do everything I could to return to heaven and see her.

⚘ ⚘

I wiped my tears and swallowed hard after the last amen. I stood next to Dad with my arms folded—keeping all the emotions I had felt during Mom's funeral on the inside where they belonged.

I again felt empty and devoid of life as I accompanied my dad and siblings out of the chapel into the noonday April sunshine. I felt heavy as we walked to the limousine behind the black hearse that would take Mom to the cemetery where her mom and dad were buried.

We'd visited that cemetery with Mom often, bearing gifts of lilacs cut from our own backyard. We gathered wild asparagus next to the stream at the top of the hill overlooking the cemetery and the entire valley. We enjoyed many brilliant sunsets from that same hill as Mom sat with all her children and told us stories of Grandma Eva making jam and Grandpa Rowley herding sheep. The sky would turn a brilliant pink, and then orange, red, and purple as the sun shared its last rays of the day with the world—reflecting its dimming light on the lake at the other side of the valley.

Mom's sunshine had dimmed prematurely, darkening my world. I could only see shadows.

I sat next to the window in the limousine and stared blankly at the throngs of people who streamed to their cars and turned on their headlights in the middle of the day—as if the headlights could cast away the shadows. But I remained dark, and empty, and alone.

I felt enclosed in a prison—trapped like a criminal who was being whisked away in a police car from the scene of a crime. Only this scene was in slow motion. People stared at me, but I looked through them, unable to focus my eyes on anything or anyone.

I was silent on the slow drive to the cemetery, hypnotized by the passing trees and white lines. Finally, the limousine stopped behind the hearse on a familiar dirt road next to the little white building with the green roof that overlooked Grandma and Grandpa's graves.

With great effort, I pulled myself out of the car. I was in time to see my six uncles carry Mom's casket down the hill like soldiers in solemn reverence. In unison, they hoisted the casket up and placed it on green straps laid on top of a deep cement vault—a vault that ensured no one would ever see Mom again. A prison like the one I felt encased in.

The dirt road that encircled the cemetery was soon lined with cars carrying crowds of people from the church to join Dad in paying their final respects to Mom. The flowers they brought encircled the cement vault as if to brighten the path to hell.

I felt lost in a crowd of adults until Jackie, my favorite cousin, found me. Like a twin, she wore a long white angel dress too. She told me how sorry she was and how sad she felt. With folded arms, I looked down at the grass and felt hollow except for the rocks that tried to fill the hole in my heart. My favorite cousin, who I'd laughed with and eaten ice cream with after my star performance just four nights earlier, seemed eternities away. We would never again be like twins—she still had a mom.

⚜ ⚜

At the conclusion of the graveside prayer, I wanted to run as far away as possible—to the other side of the earth, if I could. People were talking and laughing as if life could just go on, but I remained numb—an onlooker somewhere between the living and the dead.

Mom's casket still sat on the green straps like a monument to death, ready to be lowered into the deep, dark grave as soon as the last car pulled away. The sun would never shine on her again.

Would she remain forever trapped beneath layers of earth and stone, or would she rise again as promised by the bishop? What did that even mean? How could the dead escape a closed casket lowered in a cement vault covered with dirt?

That question haunted my dreams for years. I often awoke soaked in sweat, having dreamed that I was running for my life from my mother's ghost, who was bent on dragging me to hell too. I hated death—or maybe how this life was punctuated by death. I feared death, and I was terrified of the ghosts that haunted me when the sun went down.

"Wendy, let's go back to the church," Dad said. He grabbed Drew's hand and led us to the long, lonely car. I followed Dad up the hill and looked over my shoulder one last time at Mom's casket alone with the flowers.

I was all grown-up now, and I felt shut off from the rest of the world—the world where twelve-year-old girls still laughed and giggled about boys, tried on each other's first bras, experimented with makeup, and dreamed about Prince Charming riding up on a white horse to take them away.

I heard myself talk with family and friends at the luncheon, but I didn't feel like me. It was as if I too were floating above my body and looking down on the world. While my friends planned the next sleepover, I thought about forever. A forever without Mom. A forever of being different. A forever of being alone. Forever forever. Swirling shades of black and gray forever.

"Children, come and stand by me for a picture," Dad coaxed. I mechanically obeyed, but I couldn't force a smile. A family picture without Mom? Who would fix Annie's hair or tuck Drew's shirt in? Who would stand next to Dad? Who would fill the hole—and the hole in my heart?

The last time we took family pictures was just three weeks earlier on Easter Sunday—the day we celebrated the resurrection of Jesus, who died for us so we could live again. *Will Mom live again?* I wondered. *Will I hear her voice again, smell her perfume, feel her hands on my shoulders, and see her eyes looking into my soul? Will I taste her whole wheat bread or carrot pudding? Will I hug her again?* These are questions I ask myself even now.

With the casket closed and buried deep in the earth, how would I remember her face? She was so far away—worlds and eternities away. Would I remember her goodness, or would I be forever haunted by her ghost?

After the luncheon, we piled into the VW bus with Dad and rode back to the cemetery. The crowds were gone, and so was the casket. All that remained was a pile of flowers deliberately arranged to mark the ground where Mom slept—her body encased in a tomb covered with dirt to bury the sadness and topped with flowers to hide the pain.

I studied the flowers and tried to bury my own sadness. I carefully chose three pink roses to keep as a reminder of Mom's goodness, beauty, and life. I placed those roses in a glass box to protect her memory, preserving them in their own tomb. Over time, those roses withered and faded, like my memory of Mom. Eventually, they crumbled away altogether. Ashes to ashes, dust to dust.

11

Just Twelve, But

All Grown Up

H old on tight—here we go!" Lisa yelled over her shoulder. I lurched
backwards as I grabbed onto her waist for dear life. We raced up
the side of a steep mountain and then back down again on Lisa's powerful motorcycle.

Laurie and Ronette watched as we returned to the bottom of the
trail. Although Laurie was Lisa's older sister, she was a bit more cautious
on the mountain terrain. As soon as Lisa and I were back down safely,
Laurie, with Ronette holding on, shot up the hill, not wanting to be
outdone by her sister who was a year younger. Ronette and I idolized
Lisa and Laurie and their endless energy. We wanted to be like them
when we finally got to high school. For now, we were glad they let us
tag along.

"Laurie, I'll race you," Lisa called. We sped down the dirt road
toward an abandoned mine shaft that Cary and I used to explore. I hung
on tight with my knees to prevent torpedoing off the back. I squinted in
the sunshine, and the wind whipped my face and blew through my hair,
taking with it all my sadness, pain, and fear. Freedom!

I loved the mountains behind our house. Whether it was motorcy-
cling with friends, hiking with family, or striking out on my own, the
mountains seemed magical to me. I dreamed of long-ago places and

pretended I was a pioneer or an explorer, packing a lunch and carrying a canteen over my shoulder while I hiked for hours at a time. If you got up early enough, you could see the sun rise above the majestic, rocky peaks. The mountains were a fortress that protected me from all the troubles of the world.

There were all sorts of treasures hidden in those mountains—old glass bottles, pieces of rusted metal, seashells, and beautiful rocks of all shapes and sizes that I would take home and polish until they glistened yellow or pink or green. Some even had flecks of gold in them.

Mom knew the names of all sorts of plants, and I looked for them whenever I hiked, especially for what I thought was comfrey, a plant with fuzzy rabbit ear leaves and secret healing powers. Mom was convinced that comfrey could cure almost anything—it could knit together broken bones and heal bruises and deep cuts. As far as Mom was concerned, it was a must-have item in everyone's first aid kit. She even made comfrey poultices for our dog, Torie, when she got hit by a truck and broke her hip.

Like an experienced nurse, Mom had carefully wrapped Torie's hip with a bandage soaked in the same green comfrey goop she hid in Torie's dog food. Before long, though, our collie was up and running around in our back yard as if nothing had happened. Soon she was the proud mama of a litter of puppies—definitely a miracle!

Cary knew even more about plants than I did, but he was most interested in the little creepy crawly things that lived in the mountains—bugs, spiders, butterflies, frogs, and snakes. One day, after hiking with his friends, Cary came home and proudly showed off a prized find: a long rattlesnake with its head stuck in Cary's canteen. The snake wiggled and squirmed, shaking the rattles on the end of his tail.

Since Dad was still at work, Mom called the bishop and asked him to come and kill Cary's new pet. "Cary, you need to move out of the way," the bishop instructed as he placed the canteen on our front lawn, a flat-edged hoe ready in his hands.

With tears in his eyes, Cary begged Mom not to let the bishop kill the snake, but she insisted that it had to be. Cary sat cross-legged on the lawn just a few feet away from the deadly creature as the snake slithered out of the canteen.

The snake coiled up and wickedly rattled his tail. "Cary, move back!" I exclaimed. Cary didn't budge.

Just as the snake straightened his head in Cary's direction, ready to attack, the bishop thrust the hoe into the snake, cutting off the venomous head in one powerful blow. The head plopped down, and the body whipped around uncontrollably for a few seconds while Cary remained cross-legged on the ground like a Buddhist statue—and cried.

The bishop picked up the head with the hoe and tossed it far away on the grass, out of Cary's reach. He then straightened out the body and chopped off the rattlers, which he gave to Cary as a trophy.

Although my disheartened brother didn't understand why he couldn't keep a rattlesnake caged in his bedroom, he picked up the rattlers and inspected them. He shook them to make sure they still rattled and then carefully placed them in a glass jar to be preserved as one of his mountain treasures.

Today, on the back of Lisa's motorcycle, I wasn't looking for treasures of glass or shells or jeweled stones. I simply wanted to fly far away into the sky, where I could feel the light of the sun shining down to warm my soul, and where I could finally breathe, unencumbered by images of death.

Heaven felt closer in the mountains. God's throne must rest on the highest pinnacle of the tallest mountain in the universe so he can look down and shine his light on all of us. I wanted to fly to that throne.

And fly I did on the back of Lisa's motorcycle. I was glad to trade my white dress for jeans and a T-shirt and escape with Ronette to Kathy's home. Lisa and Laurie rescued us from the oppressive funeral crowds, the heavy rocks in my heart, and the flowers on top of a freshly dug grave.

We flew on the backs of Kathy's angel daughters. And for a moment, I remembered what it was like to be twelve again.

❧ ❧

Sunday, April 20, 1975

"Wendy, I'm leaving for morning meetings," Dad hollered down the stairs before he walked out the door. That was my cue to hurry and get the kids ready for church—fix breakfast, wipe faces, comb hairs, and dress in church clothes. After all, life must go on—even without Mom.

Cary wasn't usually much help around the house or with the other kids when Mom and Dad weren't home. He liked to tease and pester and play. But this morning he was quiet and mostly stayed in his room with his rats, gently holding one of them in his lap. Even though Cary seemed to stuff everything about Mom's death down deep inside, I think he could talk to his pets, and I'm sure they comforted him with their warmth.

Marie, on the other hand, willingly helped with Drew and Annie and continued to radiate sunshine despite burying Mom just the day before. I got Annie out of her crib, changed her diaper, and heated up a bottle while Marie skipped down the stairs to get breakfast for herself and Drew.

I joined Marie and Drew in the kitchen, Annie on my hip, and pulled off the high chair tray with one hand. Annie was usually a happy, smiley baby, but this morning she was cranky and wanted more than a bottle. I tried to quiet her with a banana, which she squished between her fingers, and some cheerios, which she dropped on the floor. Finally, I got some food inside her and cleaned her up so I could dress her in her frilly blue Sunday dress and her black patent leather shoes.

"Can you watch Annie so I can get ready for church?" I handed Annie to Marie, who was barely able to hold her up. I was exhausted because I hadn't slept well the night before—my head raced with thoughts of Mom's casket, flowers, and blood—but this morning, I was in charge, so I pushed aside those thoughts and bounded down the stairs to my basement bedroom.

I was glad to find Cary sitting on his bed outside my door as I changed one more time into my white angel dress and put one of Mom's necklaces around my neck. Cary offered protection from the ghosts that lurked in the shadows—the ghosts that had called Mom's name just four days earlier.

❧ ❧

At church, I tried to keep the kids quiet at the back of the chapel. To anyone who wasn't familiar with our situation, we must have looked like an unruly bunch of orphans, but to the rest of the congregation, we were the subject of pitiful stares and whispers—the kids whose mom had shot herself just days before and whose dad sat on the stand as a stoic example of righteous priesthood service despite his pain. Marie stayed on the bench and colored with Drew to keep him quiet. Cary sat with his arms folded, looking down at the floor. Every now and then he poked Marie. Annie kept trying to run up to Dad on the stand, so I took her to the foyer just outside the chapel doors.

Once in the foyer, Annie squirmed to get out of my arms. I let her toddle down the hall and into the gym, where her shoes clicked on the shiny floor. The accordion door that separated the last row of the chapel from the wide-open gym was closed, and the chairs that had lined the gymnasium floor just yesterday had been neatly put away, hiding all physical evidence of the funeral.

The gym was now Annie's big playroom. She had just mastered walking, and she stumbled when she tried to look over her shoulder to make sure I was right behind her. She plopped to the ground and delighted in pounding the hardwood floor with her fist like it was a toy drum. She fell to her back and giggled, showing all eight of her teeth through her big, wide smile as I swooped down to tickle her. Now that Mom was gone, she was mine, and I needed to protect her.

I heard the prelude to the last song through the closed accordion doors, so I slipped back into the chapel and held Annie on my lap next to Marie and Drew. I tried to get Annie to fold her arms during the closing prayer, but she wanted to play patty-cake instead. As soon as the concluding Amen was said and the organ started playing postlude music, Annie wiggled off my lap again. I grabbed her hand and let her guide me through the now open chapel doors.

As I looked at all the mothers guiding their children out of the chapel, I knew I was different. My mother was gone, buried beneath layers of cold earth. But I pushed down my loneliness and pain, put another rock on the pile in my heart, and gave a half-smile to the old lady who lived next door as we walked out into the April sunshine.

"Hey, Wendy, are you coming to the fireside tonight?" asked Brad, the police chief's son.

I had forgotten about the evening youth meeting, but I wanted to see my friends, so I replied, "Sure thing!" as I put Annie in her buggy. Dad would have meetings until late in the afternoon, and I still needed to get lunch for the kids, but hopefully Dad would be home before the fireside started so I could go hang out with the rest of the church youth. For now, I pushed Annie home in her buggy and coaxed the rest of the kids to follow. I was grown-up—and twelve—all at the same time.

12

Darkness Falls,
I am Dark

"Can I give you a ride home, Wendy?" Donny offered at the conclusion of the fireside that night.

"Nah, I'm walking home with Brad and Brad," I replied.

"Oh, come on," Donny teased, "Am I being turned down by a twelve-year-old?"

I giggled and turned bright red. Deep down, I wanted to ride with Donny, but Brad and Brad were some of my best friends. I liked hanging out with them, and I was happy to be a part of their group even though I was so different.

It was nearly dark when we got home—time to start getting ready for bed because there was school in the morning. I didn't have a mom to remind me it was getting late, though, so I sat on the cold front lawn with both Brads. We talked about school and summer plans and other kids—not about Mom.

I was glad to stay outside and lose myself in laughter and gossip and teasing fun. Cute Brad had stealthily picked a big pile of grass while we were talking. "Hey, Wendy," he said, and then he tossed it right in my face.

That meant all-out war.

Although I was two years younger, I could hold my own against these boys—and I wasn't afraid to fight hard. I gathered up my own weapons, tearing out the grass as fast as possible. I pulled at Brad's collar to dump the grass down his shirt and kicked off my sandals so I could run faster, heading straight for red-headed Brad's yard next door.

I was pretty fast, but Brad and Brad cornered me and ganged up on me, blinding me with fistfuls of grass torpedoes in the face. I screamed with laughter and dove onto the ground. I flailed my arms and legs, trying to protect myself from their grass bombs as they continued attacking.

Finally, next-door Brad's mom came to my rescue. She poked her head out of their partially opened front door, trying to hide her night-gown and bathrobe. "Brad," she said quietly, "It's time to come on in and get ready for bed." That was our cue that the fun was over.

"Good night, guys," I said, and then I ran to my own front door. The house was quiet and dark when I snuck in and headed to my base-ment bedroom. On the way, I realized that I was still cold from running around barefoot in the damp grass, so I turned around and headed upstairs to take a warm bath. Everyone else was in bed, so I wouldn't have to fight for the bathtub. I could relax for the first time in days.

I closed the bathroom door and locked it, just like my mom had done just four days earlier. I looked up to see if I could tell where the bullet escaped through the ceiling and out the roof. Nothing. Every-thing was in perfect order.

Determined, I took a deep breath and pushed aside thoughts of Mom. I filled the tub almost to overflowing with steamy water and stepped into heaven. Slowly, I sank into the warmth that enveloped me and protected me from the cold of the past four days. I closed my eyes for a moment and exhaled all my worries and heartaches and fears. How I loved hot baths!

After relishing the warmth for a brief minute, I reached over and closed the shower curtain to protect myself from little eyes that might try to peek under the door. In an instant, my heart stopped, my body turned ice cold, and I sat frozen in the tub face-to-face with death. Five inches away, blood splatters on the shower curtain told the tale of the grizzly deed.

I couldn't move. I couldn't breathe. The room spun as I relived the horror of that forever-ago morning. I wanted to throw up, I wanted to run, and I wanted to die all at the same time. But there I sat frozen—my heart pounding as darkness enveloped me.

Trembling, I pulled back the curtain. My eyes darted around the room, making sure I was still alone. With great effort, I lifted myself from the tub and stood naked on the rug—alone and unprotected—water dripping from my now shivering body.

I discovered more blood splatters on the wall next to the tub and a brown ring around the base of the toilet—evidence missed in the cover-up when the bathroom was scoured, the roof repaired, and the bath rug sanitized and replaced in the exact spot where Mom must have lain, her lifeless body never to breathe again.

I looked on the shelf below the bathroom mirror, and I saw weapons. I imagined Mom stabbing herself with the sharp end of her eyebrow comb or slicing herself with her razor, filling the tub with her red blood. And now ghosts invaded my waking hours just as they had my dreams.

I felt haunted, alone, and terrified. It was dark outside. I was dark.

13

The First Bandage Removed

My heart pounded as I waited in silence for John's reply. "You can't replace your mom, can you, Wendy?" he said slowly, apparently moved by my description of Mom's death. A bullet that ripped through her pink nightgown and out the roof. A bullet that left a gaping hole in my heart.

I shook my head no and waited through another long pause.

"I'm sorry," John finally said, looking at me with thoughtful eyes. He looked like a heart surgeon examining a patient dying from congestive heart failure. But unlike a surgeon who might try to play God with open-heart surgery, John didn't pretend that he could take the pain away. Instead, he gave me an assignment that would inflict more pain and fear and terror.

He described an event in his own childhood where he had played with matches and burned his arm. John had hidden the burn from his mom so he wouldn't get in trouble. When his mom finally discovered the burn, it was infected. She took John immediately to the doctor who, although it was very painful, scraped off the infection, cleansed the wound, and dressed it with ointment and clean gauze so that it could heal properly.

I thought of the traumatic third-degree burns my mom had endured as a child. Her sisters described hardly being able to listen to her cries and begged to not have to change the bandages. Mom's burns had finally healed, though they'd left deep scars.

John explained that in order to heal properly, I would need to rip off the layers of old, infected bandages that were wrapped around my heart—what I hadn't done when I was twelve. I would need to pull out the dirt and rocks that were now embedded there and scrub and rinse and disinfect the wound before I could apply the balm that would soothe and comfort and heal my broken heart. Surely, like my mom's burns, I would still have a scar, but I could uncover my heart and laugh and cry and share and connect. I could become whole again and fill my heart with light instead of darkness. John asked me to trust him and take a step into that darkness. He lit a single candle to show the way.

"Do you think you could read that journal entry to a couple of people you trust?" John asked. It was a terrifying thought. Did I have anyone close enough to reveal a secret I had carefully protected? What would they think? Would they condemn me? Would they judge me? Would they hurt me? He explained that talking about something I had kept buried for so many years was the first step to healing.

"Okay," I hesitantly agreed. "I could do that." I had carried these rocks and worn a glass mask for nearly four decades. My shoulders were weary. My face was cold. My heart hurt. I was willing to remove that mask, rip off the bandages, dig out the rocks, and share and love and cry with someone else instead of crying alone in the bathroom with the water running.

Who could I share it with? I asked myself over the next several days of painting on my smile and going to work. I was the nurse manager of sixty-five nurses and nursing assistants at our local hospital. I had been in nursing leadership for fifteen years and, by all appearances, I was a driven, put-together, goal-oriented, outcomes-focused high achiever.

I loved mentoring new nurses and aides who had their whole bright futures ahead of them, and I relished in their success as much as I did in my own. I loved my employees like they were my children, but like my own children, they knew very little about my past. They knew nothing about the hole in my heart that needed cleansing.

Two employees radiated light with their care and concern of others, and I determined that if I could trust anyone, I could trust these two— Blake and Melissa.

Melissa was a soft-spoken mom who, although she wanted to stay at home with her four young boys instead of working full time, was a talented educator. She was my right arm in the nursing unit's leadership. She welcomed new employees with a soft approach that helped them feel like a valued part of our work family. She listened with empathy and understanding and gently corrected when needed. Melissa was my sounding board—she listened without judgment when I shared my frustrations about employees or physicians, and she offered support when I was devastated at William's early return from his mission. I knew I could trust her with my secret.

Blake was a gentle man with a tender heart. He didn't hide his emotions when he talked about the health challenges of his dear wife and children. Supporting and caring for them were his top priorities, and that love was reciprocated—his wife had supported him through the sudden death of his own mother just a few years earlier.

Blake's mom and dad loved hiking and climbing mountains together. They were both experienced climbers who taught their children the magic of adventure in God's expansive world. One day Blake's mom and dad went hiking by themselves in the beautiful backcountry of Utah's Escalante National Monument. They went up and over the red and yellow rocks and came to a narrow crevice and decided to explore.

Blake's dad was holding the rope for his mom as she rappelled down the narrow hole when the unthinkable happened—she slipped and broke her shoulder, landing in a pool of water at the bottom. With her shoulder broken, Blake's mom couldn't pull herself out of the water and, although his dad used every ounce of energy he could and prayed with all his might, he was unable to lift her.

Over the next several hours, as hypothermia set in, they both knew that she would die in that hole with her husband on the other end of the rope, unable to save her life. They shared their never-ending love for each other. Then Blake's mom, too weak to keep her head out of the water any longer, succumbed to that dark, cold, watery grave.

At her funeral, I learned of her love for her family and their adoration for her. Blake was devastated at the tragic loss of his own angel mom but comforted in knowing she died doing what she loved with her husband.

"Blake, do you have a few minutes to talk with me?" I asked him one morning. He followed me into my office. After some small talk, I summoned my courage and haltingly said, "Um . . . I'm working on some things related to . . . um . . . my mom's death when I was twelve, and . . . um . . . would you—would you mind if I read you something from my journal?"

Blake looked a little confused by my request, so I explained, "It's part of my therapy."

"Uh, sure," Blake said, uncertain where I was headed with this conversation.

"If I could cry enough tears to take away the pain . . . ," I started. I swallowed, then continued, "When Mom leaned over the gun, as Dad described, in her pink nightgown, and pulled the trigger—" I didn't look up. I couldn't—not until I had finished the assignment. "Mom shot each of her children when she shot herself—and a piece of us died with her."

I nervously looked up and met Blake's tear-filled eyes. "I had no idea, Wendy," he said, clearly moved. He understood the raw pain of losing one's mother and unashamedly shared in the sorrow I had hidden away for so many years.

"I know how hard it is to lose a mom, Wendy, but I can't imagine how hard this must be for you," he continued. "How do you do it? How do you do all that you do? How are you as successful as you are with all you've been through?"

I shrugged my shoulders. I wasn't sure how to answer. *I was the oldest. I had to grow up. I had to be strong. Life goes on, doesn't it?*

I didn't feel successful. I was just trying to survive—so I'd buried the pain and put on a glass face. But now the tears escaped. I'd taken off the first layer of dirty old bandages and lifted up the mask for a minute.

❧ ❦

Over the next few days, I fought an internal debate. *Oh my gosh, what have I done?* I asked myself as I read and reread the journal entry I'd shared with Blake.

I had started to peel off the bandages and had let out a few of the pebbles, but part of me wanted to snatch them back and bury them in my heart again, horrified that I had let the secret slip. The other part of me wanted to rip off the rest of the bandages and get a bulldozer to dig out the piles of rocks and uncover my heart.

Because my heart was so tightly bandaged, I couldn't feel love. I felt emptiness. Nothingness.

In an attempt to understand death, I had read about the near-death experiences of several people in a book called *Life after Life*. A universal experience of those who died of natural causes included going to a bright light—to a being of light who asked how they had loved in their mortal lives on earth. Love seemed to be a prerequisite to entering heaven.

I asked John once during a therapy session, "How can I make it to heaven if I don't feel love? Does it count in heaven if I do loving things but I don't feel love?"

I wanted to feel again. I wanted to feel joy and happiness and light and love instead of never-ending sadness. So I determined to share my journal entry again, this time with Melissa, my angel educator.

"Melissa, can I talk with you?" I asked.

"Of course. What's up?" she replied as she sat down next to me in my office.

Melissa was my best friend at work, and she knew I was seeing a therapist. She also knew some of my family secrets and was a constant support for me.

"I met with John this week, and one of my therapy assignments is to share a part of my journal with a few people," I explained. "Would you mind if I read it to you?"

"Not at all," she replied.

"Okay, let me see if I can find it," I said as I nervously thumbed through the pages of the yellow college-ruled notebook where I had recorded my most intimate thoughts and fears.

"I should have marked where it was," I muttered as I flipped page after page. I only wanted to share the prescribed description of Mom's death. I didn't want Melissa to see my private rantings of a few weeks ago, January 2011.

John had given me an earlier assignment to think about all the ways my life had been impacted because my mom shot herself. As I lifted the bandage to take a peek, it was as if I'd stepped back in time. I was twelve again.

I had written:

> *Am I crazy?*
>
> *My brain is fuzzy—wired backwards. I can't think straight. But I have to—people are counting on me. I need to be strong!*
>
> *I am tired. I have to go on. But I am so tired. I want peace. I want connection. Will four visits heal a lifetime of pain?*

I don't want to be alone.
I want my mom!

My writing screamed on the page.

It hurts. I am sad.
I can't stop crying. Oh my gosh, what have I done to open this up?
Tear open the wounds and scrub harder, to use John's analogy. Why?
Where is God? Isn't the Savior supposed to heal? Where is He? There
is no one to answer my prayers or hear my cries.
I am alone!

But here I sat with a wonderful friend. Not alone. An angel on earth sent from God, who sometimes felt so distant.

"Mom shot each of her children when she shot herself—and a piece of us died with her."

I finished reading the passage and looked up to meet Melissa's tear-filled eyes. My own eyes remained dry, but my heart opened just a little bit more, and I received Melissa's love and compassion.

"I would love to see a picture of your mom," Melissa said as we talked more about her life and love. "She seems wonderful."

A knock interrupted the moment, but before opening my office door, I stood and accepted Melissa's warm embrace.

"Thanks for listening," I said.

"Thanks for trusting me," she answered.

❧ ❧

Later the next day, Melissa came to check on me. I was prepared with a bag full of my dad's personal history—his life story and two spiral-bound books containing hundreds of my parents' high school love letters, written between 1957 and 1960. They wrote during their classes and after school and exchanged their letters on the windowsill of Mom's bedroom window. These letters were priceless. They gave me a glimpse into Mom and Dad's early relationship, their insecurities, their jealousies, their fights, and their love.

One undated entry written by my mom reads:

Hi Handsome,

Well, Wally, first thing I have to say is I'm terribly sorry for not call-
ing you tonight. To be truthful, the reason I didn't is just because I forgot.
Honey, I am truly sorry for it too. . . .

Well, it is about 9:45 and I haven't taken a bath or put up my hair, so I will do that after you come for this letter. So, I'll be getting to bed a little later. . . .

Wally, I just can't tell you how much I have missed you tonight, and Honey, I know that my love is growing for you every day. I can remember when I didn't know for sure whether or not I loved you, I do now. I know it Darling, although I still can't say that I know I'll marry you for sure, but I will be able to some day, you know. Gee, Hon, I hope you get to bed early tonight, by 11:00, say. We'll surprise each other tomorrow by not knowing what each other is wearing, okay?

Well, Wally, I had better close now as you will be here before long. I'm going to try and be bathed before you get here. If I'm not by the window, you know where I'll be. So don't be angry just in case I'm not out of the tub.

Love Forever, Linda (dimples, blonde, Lynny, beautiful)

P.S. I love you, honey. Be sure and be in bed by 11:00.

This fourteen-year-old Linda dared suggest to my dad in her letters what he should wear, what time to go to bed, and even when he should go to the dentist. She loved him, but she wasn't sure about the marriage thing. Her letters went back and forth between loving my dad and not being sure about her love for him or apologizing for being "snotty" to him. And Dad desperately wanted her to commit to marry him when she graduated from high school. Dad wrote:

I hope my love will always mean a great deal to you. I know yours does to me and always will, as long as you keep loving me.

I proudly showed Melissa the histories and the many pictures of my beautiful young mom. I talked with her about Mom's love and energy and spunk. I talked about her laughter. Then I talked about her illness. And her death.

In his Easter letter of 1958, Dad wrote:

You are the only one for me. I hope that I'll never lose you. That is the day I am fearing most. You mean more than anything else to me.

Sadly, Dad's greatest fear was realized seventeen years later.

I cried as I shared the letters with Melissa. And as hard as I tried to stuff it back in, I couldn't hold back the tears any longer. "I don't know why I'm crying," I stammered.

"Wendy, it's okay to cry." Melissa comforted me like an angel mom. "Sometimes you get so full of pain you just have to let some of it out. It's all you can hold."

I felt love. And my heart opened.

14

Who Will Save Me Now?

Losing a mom to suicide at twelve brings indescribable challenges—alterations to your very being. The foundation upon which you have relied for your very life has crumbled beneath you, and you feel stuck in a sea of swirling darkness—quicksand that tries to suffocate you as it pulls you to the center of the earth, to be buried with the one you love more than life itself—but you didn't get the chance to tell her that. You were only a child!

You bargain with God to bring her back, to undo what has been done. You think of all the ways you could—*should*—have saved her. "If only I hadn't begged for ice cream." You carry guilt that isn't yours to carry, and you remain helpless. You remain dead.

Suicide of a loved one at any age brings with it unimaginable pain, and you think you might die from the crushing weight on your chest that threatens to keep your heart from beating. Sometimes you even count your heartbeats to make sure you're still alive.

Your mom is supposed to protect you—to save you from the monsters lurking around the corner as she tucks you in bed every night. Your mom reminds you to take your vitamins, eat your vegetables, brush your teeth, wash your hands, and say your prayers. Your mom is supposed to love you.

But when your mom shoots herself, you question that love. You question your very existence. You question whether you're lovable at all. If you were, then why did she pull the trigger?

You question if there really is a God.

When your mom shoots herself instead of protecting you, she becomes the monster lurking in the dark.

※ ※

SPRING 1975

"Wendy, what are you doing up there?" Cindy asked, clearly afraid I had gone completely mad. "Get down here now!" she yelled.

But I wouldn't budge. I *couldn't* budge.

Cindy was one of my best friends. She was a whole head taller than the rest of the girls and two heads taller than the boys in seventh grade—definitely someone you could be afraid of, but she had a heart of gold. Cindy made a great Injun Joe when we played Daniel Boone hunting bears and mountain lions—before the seventh grade, that is.

Cindy loved listening to me play the piano and sing, something I did often since Mom died. I could escape in my music and find comfort in the words of hymns or love songs, and Cindy would sit for hours as an audience of one.

When grown-ups heard me play, they often said, "Your mom would be so proud." I would give them a half smile and continue playing, wishing my mom could see me and clap for me. Would she finally really be proud of me? Would she want to stay? Would she love me?

I knew Cindy could rescue me if I was ever trapped or hurt. She was like my own personal bodyguard, fearless and unstoppable. But now she was scared. I clung to the rafters in the garage, refusing to come down.

I was scared too. My brain wasn't working right, and I thought I would be the next to die. The ghosts of my dreams—the ghosts that would lead me down to hell—haunted me through the day now too, with thoughts of sharp combs, razors, and a blood-filled tub.

I was terrified of death, afraid of the dark, and obsessed with my own mortality. And I hung to the rafters for dear life, afraid to move.

I had found a spot on my chest that was getting bigger and changing shape, and I knew that it was a death sentence for me. I found the spot while I was showering before Mom died, but I'd never talked to her about it. My mom thought she had cancer before she shot herself, so naturally I knew I had cancer too. I looked up cancer in the encyclopedia, and, sure enough, a change in a mole was one of the four signs of cancer. Now I had retreated to the rafters to escape death.

I felt crazy. There was so much darkness and fear and death that I couldn't think straight. I wanted to scream—at Cindy, at my dad, at my mom, even at God. But instead, I sat frozen in the rafters, unable to move, talk, or breathe.

Since she couldn't talk me into retreating from my hiding place, Cindy finally left me alone while I clutched the splintered wooden rafters and braced myself with my legs. I sat there thinking of cold, dark death.

"Wendy," a kind voice spoke from the ground below, "It's time to come down."

I looked down and saw Kathy looking up at me, concern on her face. Afraid for my safety and not knowing what to do or how to rescue me, Cindy had run to Kathy to save me from certain death.

I reluctantly agreed to let go of the rafters and swung down onto the orange boat parked in the garage—the boat I used to help Mom clean and wax. That boat was the center of our weekend family outings. Only we weren't a family anymore. Mom would never ski from that boat again.

I looked at my feet as Kathy walked me into the house. I slouched in embarrassment as she sat with me on the green-and-pink velvety couch where Mom had told me about the tumor growing inside of her. It was the same couch where I'd sat when I'd learned Mom had died.

"Wendy, just because your mom died doesn't mean you will," Kathy tried to explain as I sat with my elbows on my knees, my face resting on closed fists, and my head bowed.

My mind barely registered Kathy's words as it raced from bullets to blood to razors to tumors to moles and back to bullets. Death was everywhere. Mom wasn't old—she wasn't even a grandma. If she could die, then certainly I could too.

"I know it's scary, Wendy," Kathy went on, "but you're not going to die."

I finally looked up and caught the love and concern in Kathy's eyes. It was just a moment, and then I looked back down at the worn green carpet.

My foundation was gone. My mom, who used to bandage my scraped knees when I fell off my bike and pick the gravel out of my hands and rub aloe vera on my blistered sunburns, couldn't comfort me anymore. She couldn't remove the fear from my mind or heart. She couldn't tell me everything would be okay. She couldn't tell me she loved me. She left me. She shot me!

"Wendy, you're not going to die!" Kathy said again with emphasis.

"Okay," I nodded after a minute. "I know."

I tried to know, anyway. But I spent the next four decades battling primitive, haunting fears of the dark, ghosts, guns, knives, and diseases. I was afraid of death. I was terrified.

❧ ❧

Kathy tried to step in and fill a huge void. Besides being my youth leader at church, she welcomed me into her home and into her heart—and I cautiously accepted her embrace.

"Wendy, would you like to spend the night?" Kathy asked shortly after Mom died. "Lisa and Laurie will be home, and we can watch movies and eat chocolate." Kathy smiled.

"Sure," I heard myself say. I watched myself go through the motions of living, but I felt separated from those around me—separated from life.

Although Kathy did everything to make certain I felt welcomed, I didn't feel like I belonged anywhere. Nighttime was especially hard. I smiled, though, and pretended to enjoy myself. I pretended that everything was okay.

That night, Laurie let me sleep in her big double bed in her room. After brushing my teeth, changing into my pajamas, and telling Kathy good night, I went downstairs to Laurie's bedroom, turned off the light, and climbed into an unfamiliar bed in an unfamiliar bedroom and listened to the unfamiliar sounds of a dark, unfamiliar basement.

I must have been exhausted because I fell right to sleep. The next thing I remember, Laurie was sitting by my bedside, gently shaking my shoulder as I lay sweating in bed, moaning for my mom.

"Wendy, are you okay?" Laurie asked, anxious and concerned.

I couldn't move. I was shivering, and the heavy blankets were soaked with my sweat. Laurie touched my forehead as I lay there, unable to lift my head from the pillow.

"You're burning up," she said. "I'm going to get my mom."

I cried a silent cry and wished for my own mom to comfort me. I watched myself in my aloneness as I lay there in the dark in someone else's bed. Stabbing pains of homesickness pierced my heart, and tears welled up in my eyes.

Mom knew just what to do whenever I was sick. She knew what herbal tea to give me and what poultice to put around my neck to draw out the infection. She knew how to nurse me back to health. But now I felt hopelessly alone and vulnerable, even as Laurie returned with a wet washcloth, and thermometer, and her mom.

"Wendy, let's check your temperature," Kathy instructed as she handed me the thermometer and Laurie put the cool cloth on my forehead.

I tried to swallow the saliva in my mouth before putting the thermometer under my tongue, but my throat felt like hot coals, and the saliva ran out of the corners of my mouth. I lay there with my eyes shut tight to keep the light away from my pounding head.

I want my mom, I thought.

Mommy? I pleaded in my mind, wishing she could reach down from heaven and take my hand.

After a few minutes, I opened my eyes just briefly when Kathy took out the thermometer and said with concern, "One hundred four point five."

Kathy and Laurie spent the next hour or so by my bedside, changing wet rags to cool me off as I shivered uncontrollably. Finally, my fever broke, and Kathy and Laurie went back to bed. I lay there in the dark, thinking of Mom and silently sobbing.

Moms are supposed to protect you. Moms are supposed to bandage your skinned knees and wipe away your tears. Moms are supposed to care for you when you're sick and comfort you when you're sad. Moms are always supposed to be there.

Moms aren't supposed to shoot themselves. They're not supposed to die.

15

Etched in Granite

Wendy, could you come with me to pick out Mom's headstone?"
Dad asked. A week ago I was Mom's right arm—now I was
Dad's. That meant babysitting and cleaning and cooking—and, I
guess, picking out headstones too. After Mom's funeral, I kept busy
with school, church activities, and sleepovers with my friends. Life
went on.

Although a lady in our church volunteered to watch the kids during
the day until Dad got home for dinner, I watched the kids on evenings
and Saturdays while he worked late to grow his business or while he
attended midweek church meetings. I also tried to keep the kids quiet
during church on Sundays and watched them after church while Dad
went to his meetings. Eventually, Dad started dating to find a new wife,
and he was gone even more.

I knew how to clean the house the way Mom had taught me and,
along with babysitting, Dad often tasked me with making sure everyone did their chores. Although Mom had taught me how to bake bread
and can peaches, I wasn't much of a cook. I did my best, but it was good
that the lady at church made dinner Monday through Friday.

Along with babysitting and cleaning and cooking, I felt especially
responsible for Annie. I took her on walks in her brown plaid buggy,
pushing her up and down the streets of our foothill neighborhood,
stopping by my friends' homes or visiting Kathy. I felt like her mom

now, and I was determined to protect her and care for her. Dad hated changing diapers, so I even took care of that. I loved her.

When I wasn't babysitting or busy with my friends, I had time to think about Mom. And I was sad. I played the guitar and the piano to ease my pain, and I wrote down some of my sad thoughts to make sense of my mom's death:

> *Who am I, and where am I going? What is my purpose here on Earth? Why did God send me here where I am, instead of someone else? Why are there so many other people who don't have homes or parents? Why am I so fortunate to be able to have a lovely home and a wonderful mother and father and such wonderful brothers and sisters? Why am I so lucky? Why? Why? Why? I wish I knew. . . .*
>
> *What is my mom's purpose in heaven? Was it meant for her to go the way she went, or what? I need to talk to someone about my problems. I need someone. I need someone who I can really talk to. . . .*
>
> *Just if I had been able to talk to my mom, maybe I would have been better off. But there are no ifs because it's over with. I'll just have to make the best of my life. I'm going to live each day as if it were my last, and just pretend that Christ is my constant companion.*

Before Mom died, if I did something she didn't approve of—like argue with my brothers or sisters or neglect my chores—she would remind me that I should do what Jesus would want me to do. So I determined that if I pretended Jesus was right there, maybe I could be perfect and see my mom again. Perfection was an awful burden for a twelve-year-old to carry—one that I could never carry on my own. But still, I placed it on my back.

I missed my mom terribly and longed for God to return her to me. I remember seeing mail that was delivered for her. She would never be able to open it. I tried to focus on the blessings I had, such as a lovely home and a wonderful mother and father and such wonderful brothers and sisters, but I still hurt inside. I longed for connection. I longed for understanding. I longed for someone to talk with.

I held in the tears until I was alone—walking in the April rain or riding my bike to the cemetery. I sat on the hillside next to Mom's grave overlooking the city and the lake. I talked to her. And I cried buckets of tears.

Why? I asked. *Why did you die? Why did you shoot yourself? Where are you? Where is God? Why?*

I cried until I could cry no more. I emptied my soul, and the emptiness remained on the silent ride back to my home, back to my life that must go on.

⚬⚬⚬

I was silent on the drive to the Beesley Monument. It was just a week after Mom died, and life was so different. Everywhere I looked there were reminders of Mom—her mail, her purse, her shoes, her perfume, her driver's license, her glasses, her coat, her bread maker and wheat grinder and sprouter, and the picture of the Last Supper that hung next to our dining room table—all reminders of a mom who should still be filling the house with her laughter and love. And yet there was silence.

Every day I came home from school half expecting the silence to be broken. I half expected to hear Mom's musical laugh and see her legs dangling over the blue chair in the kitchen while she talked on the phone with her sisters. And I jumped a little when the phone rang and the person on the end of the line asked if my mom was home.

No, she's dead! I wanted to scream. But instead I just said, "No, may I help you?" And I remained silent.

The flowers at the cemetery had faded away, so now my job was to help Dad pick out a headstone—a slab of cold, gray, heavy, lifeless granite to mark where Mom lay dead under a pile of dirt and rocks.

"What do you think about this one, Wendy?" Dad asked as we walked through the dusty, dirty, cold warehouse that housed the samples of rock etched with flowers.

Like a grown-up advisor, I shared my opinions with Dad until we settled on a beautiful flat headstone with three vases that would hold the flowers we would eternally place there. Along with a picture of the temple and date that Mom and Dad were married, Dad's name would be etched in the stone next to Mom's. The granite would forever mark Mom's final resting place and would preserve a spot for Dad next to her. I could be buried there too because Dad had bought ten extra burial plots. I shuddered at the thought.

The salesman showed us where and how they engraved the stone with sandblasters, how they covered their faces with glass masks as they aimed their gun at the carefully marked stone and blasted away. I recoiled when the gun went off.

Like the granite, my cold, dark heart was permanently etched with pain and sadness that could never be erased.

16

The Lone and Dreary World

Although I tried to cover up my sadness with my own glass face and bury the pain beneath dirt and rocks, sometimes it slipped out, not as tears but as anger—an eruption of hot rocks spewing from a volcano that could no longer contain the built-up pressure of layers of pain.

One evening, Dad asked me to help with the dishes. I'd had enough of dishes and diapers and dirt. I didn't want to clean one more thing! I hated cleaning; I hated the house; I hated life; I hated death; and I hated Dad. I finally burst. After holding in so much pain—after cleaning and babysitting and keeping kids quiet at church and cooking and pushing Annie in her buggy and picking out headstones—after crying alone at the cemetery—I exploded. I yelled and stomped and screamed and stormed.

"*I HATE YOU!*" I screamed at the top of my lungs. I ran down the stairs to my haunted room with the orange carpet and the Holly Hobbie wallpaper, slammed the door, and flung myself onto the bed. I buried my face in my pillow and sobbed and sobbed. I couldn't contain the tears anymore, and my body shook on the bed.

There was a quiet knock on the door and I yelled, "Go away!" as I tried to catch my breath.

My dad entered the room anyway and stood at the foot of my bed.

I rolled over and stared at him and shut my heart tight. No light could get in, and no tears could get out. I imprisoned my soul within my body. I clenched my teeth and folded my arms and lay frozen with my head on the pillow as he spoke.

"Wendy, I know it's hard," he said, apparently trying to understand where my rage came from. "You're getting older, and you're starting to get new hormones as you grow into a young lady."

Huh? What are you talking about? I thought as I stared at him.

"Women have changing hormones every month that sometimes make it hard for them to understand their feelings," he continued.

I was speechless as I lay there, my muscles taut, my face twitching.

You have no idea! I hate you! I thought to myself while he stumbled around with his words, trying to tell me how hard it was to grow up.

I want my mom! I screamed inside. *But my mom is dead! She shot herself!*

He didn't talk to me about Mom. He didn't talk about her death or her life. He couldn't. He talked about changing hormones. I hadn't even started my period yet and was barely in a training bra, and my dad was talking about hormones! I wasn't even sure what they were.

It was against the unspoken rules to talk about Mom, so Dad blamed hormones.

This is not hormones! I wanted to scream again. *I miss my mom!*

But instead, I stared at Dad and remained silent.

❧ ❧

School provided a routine that helped mask the pain and loneliness for the month after Mom died. I kept as busy as I could with friends, piano, cleaning, babysitting, homework, writing, visiting Kathy, and playing my guitar. But as soon as school was out for the summer, I was lost. We were all lost.

Mrs. Smith, the lady from church, was in my space—in Mom's space—all day long. She didn't clean as well as Mom or I did, but she made pretty good food, so we didn't starve. It was terribly uncomfortable, though, to give up my home to a stranger—a stranger who, by her very presence, reminded me at all times that my mom was gone.

Dad seemed lost too. Even though he stayed busy with work and church responsibilities, his face was vacant and sad. He was empty. He didn't eat; he just worked. And he still didn't say anything.

And because Dad didn't say anything, no one else did either. We just tried to survive. Ten-year-old Cary started acting up more and spent more time with some of his questionable friends. He even started drinking alcohol to dull the pain.

Seven-year-old Marie would wander the neighborhood in her bare feet, knocking on doors of the older ladies' homes to get their treats and their love. Marie told me years later that she would go into the bishop's daughter, Marci's, bathroom and put rose lotion in her hands. She would raise her hands to her face, smell the sweet fragrance, and silently weep. Mom used to wear rose water, and Marie longed for a connection to the Mom who was forever gone.

Adorable Drew did what most four-year-olds do—he ran and played and giggled and teased and hid from the adults who tried to make him take a bath. He was eleven years old when he learned how Mom died from one of his friends. He got so angry that he threw a rock through his friend's bedroom window. He wanted to burn that friend's house down to the ground. Instead, he nearly lost his own hand as he played with fire a few years later. He required skin grafts and several days in the hospital.

And darling one-year-old Annie cried and laughed and toddled. She grew up without knowing her mom, and yet, she looked exactly like Mom. She even talked like Mom. When Annie was thirteen, she learned, also from a friend, that Mom had shot herself. On April 16th of that same year—twelve years to the day that Mom shot herself—Annie tried to take her life too.

Dad didn't know how devastating his silence would be. He was just trying to survive like the rest of us.

Every summer, we had gone on a family vacation, usually with Grandma and Grandpa and always with Mom—until this summer. But still, we loaded up in the big Chinook motor home—five rowdy kids, two round grandparents, and a tired dad at the wheel—and drove and drove and drove.

Dad must have been trying to escape too, because he took us up the entire California coast from Disneyland to the California Redwoods and on to Crater Lake in Oregon. Dad and Grandpa and I took turns carrying Annie in the blue baby carrier while we walked through Chinatown in San Francisco and Grandpa taught us how to eat crab legs and shrimp from the street vendors.

We never talked about Mom, and yet she was noticeably absent. Grandma made the trip's peanut butter sandwiches on store-bought bread. Mom would have made them on homemade bread. Grandma had a hard time keeping up in Disneyland or on the beach because she was fat and her hips and knees hurt from arthritis. Mom would have been walking so fast that the rest of us would have had to run just to keep up with her. And no one really wanted to be buried in the sand next to the ocean without Mom there to rescue us. Mom was buried beneath layers of cold, dark earth.

Grandpa did try to keep things light and happy with his constant teasing. We all thought it was hilarious when he took his fake teeth out and smiled a toothless grin or when he drove with no hands and suddenly put on the air brakes. Grandpa taught us all how to fish and made us put our own squishy worms on the hook. The worms wiggled and fought even after they were pierced and their guts had splattered everywhere. Grandpa tied several hooks on one line so that we could improve our chances of catching trout right after the lake was stocked. One time we filled an entire metal washtub. Grandpa was every kid's favorite.

And Grandpa loved Mom. He missed her terribly. But he didn't talk about her either. He just tried to make the rest of us laugh instead of cry.

Grandpa didn't talk with me about Mom until years later, in a comment about Cary, who was still struggling with alcohol and had added street drugs to his numbing formula. "He would sure be a lot different now if your Mom was still alive," Grandpa said. "She loved you kids more than anything,"

And yet, she still shot herself.

Grandpa had offered the graveside prayer before the heavy casket lid was closed forever on Mom's face and memory. "Heavenly Father," he said, "please bless the children that they may find the desire and strength to live the kind of lives their mother has taught them." But she wasn't there to help us through our darkest hours. We each floundered around without even a flicker of light or hope—without our mom. We put on our own masks, and took our paths alone.

I guess we would have all been different if Mom was still alive. As it was, we each tried to conquer our individual demons in silence.

17

My Mom Is Missing

Mark, I have something to talk to you about." I had spent the two weeks after John had given me the assignment summoning all the courage I could muster. My heart was pounding, my head hurt, my hands were sweating, and I wanted to throw up.

I had already shared my journal entry with Blake and Melissa at work, but for some reason, I was terrified to share with Mark, my husband of twenty-nine years. I was afraid of opening up my heart to more hurt and pain and rejection. I was afraid of sharing what I had so carefully protected for decades.

"Okay, let's talk," Mark said as I sat on our family room couch with my yellow notebook in hand.

Mark sat next to me, and I rigidly scooted away to the other end of the couch. I put my knees to my chest and wrapped my arms tightly around them as if to keep the bandages secure and the rocks and dirt in place around my heart.

"Well?" Mark said, encouraging me to talk.

Two days before, I had shared with Mark for the first time, almost in passing, that I was working on my mom's death in therapy with John. It didn't feel like it was almost in passing to me, though, because I had anxiously thought about it for two straight weeks until I finally blurted it out. And then I was silent. And on the opposite end of the couch from Mark, I remained silent.

Finally, I thumbed through the notebook and said, "John wanted me to read this to you."

"Okay," Mark said slowly, waiting for me to continue.

"At that very moment, the same bullet pierced my heart and left a gaping hole." I read the passage to him, and in my mind I saw Mom lean over the gun. Tears filled my eyes as I finished. I couldn't contain them any longer. I cried and cried, sharing with Mark how afraid and alone and sad I felt. I shared from my bleeding, broken heart.

I was not prepared for what Mark said next. I had just borne my whole soul to my husband for the first time ever in our twenty-nine years of marriage, and he said, emotionlessly, "Why haven't you shared this with me before? Why didn't you trust me?"

I sat there stunned. I had just ripped open the bandage and exposed the hole in my heart to my husband—the man who was supposed to love me more than anyone else—and he was stomping on it. My heart was bleeding, and he didn't lovingly soak up the blood. Instead, he worried about himself. He could have just spit in my face or shot me in the heart too.

"You're worried about *you*?!" I shouted. "How dare you!"

I described the weight. I shared the whole story. I sobbed and cried and shouted about how awful it was and the impact it had on my whole life. I described the unbearable pain I continued to feel and how I would cover it up with anger. And he didn't say, "I'm so sorry you've carried this by yourself for so long." No, instead he said, "Why do you have to be angry?"

"Blake and Melissa cried with me, and you wonder why I don't trust you?" I shouted again.

Mark remained calm. He tried to put on his therapist hat with empty phrases like, "I'm sorry you're going through a hard time right now." Like this was a passing phase!

He didn't understand at all. Then he said, "I'm sure it was very frustrating."

That did it. "'I'm sure it was frustrating'?" I screamed at the top of my lungs. "'Frustrating' is what you get when you can't tie your shoes! *Frustrating?!*"

Mark tried to backpedal. "I'm trying to understand," he said. "You have a hole in yourself. Something is missing."

"Something is *missing*?!" I shouted again. And with ever-increasing volume and intensity and emotion and furor, I screamed, "I have a hole in my *HEART*! My *MOM* is missing!"

And the silence was broken.

18

Make Room for the Other Lady

July 4, 1975, was the day I met the other lady. Two and a half months after Mom died, seventy-six days after we buried her beneath the cold earth, Dad took us to the Fourth of July parade, an annual family tradition. And while the rest of the kids played with cap guns and waved American flags and watched the glistening floats streaming by, I watched as Dad met the lady he'd seen in a dream.

I watched Dad talk to this stranger—a tall, skinny lady I had never seen before with long black hair and sharp, dramatic facial features that were intense and rigid and scary and dark to me—almost witchlike. A stark contrast to my five-foot-two-inch energetic mom, who was an instant friend to all. Mom readily shared her bright smile and drew people to her with her bubbly personality. Mom was warm. This lady was not.

But Dad was enamored with this other lady and her eight-year-old daughter. And besides, the bishop had told him to go find a wife and mother for his children. I guessed I could get used to the idea. I tried to, anyway.

While Dad was out finding a replacement wife for himself, I was home with the kids doing things that moms do—sort of. I was still a kid—a preteen, nearly adolescent growing kid who invited boys over to the house while I babysat and who ran off with my friends any chance I could get.

One night, after playing night games with my friends, I ran into the house and saw my Dad sitting next to this other lady, holding hands on the green-and-pink velvety couch—Mom's couch. I hid my shock and disgust and tried to tell myself that we needed a mom. At the same time, this lady told my dad in no uncertain terms that she would *not* mother his children. But Dad had a plan for that. He would have a nanny to help with the kids—Mrs. Smith—who would fix dinner and do the laundry and play with Annie and Drew.

So Dad kept holding hands and even kissing this other lady. And I watched.

It made sense that we needed a mom—children need moms—but I wanted my own mom back. I didn't want this other lady to sit on my mom's couch or eat at my mom's table or sleep in my mom's bed!

But my mom was gone forever.

So I played the piano, wrote songs on the guitar, pushed Annie in her buggy, visited Kathy, and cried alone in my bedroom.

One day while I was playing the piano for Cindy and singing our favorite music, I hit a particularly high note, and my glasses cracked right down the middle of one of the lenses. Cindy and I both had a good laugh over my shattered glasses, but Dad was too busy with the other lady to notice.

He was also too busy with the other lady to notice when one of the temples on my glasses snapped off. Since I couldn't see ten feet away without them and since they wouldn't stay on my face, I tied a shoelace to my glasses and wrapped it around my head, hooking the other end on the remaining temple. I cinched up the shoelace and keep my glasses from falling off. I looked out of glasses with one cracked lens and a shoelace dangling in front of the other.

I went to girls' camp that summer with my cracked glasses tied on with a shoestring, but it really wasn't cool to start eighth grade that way, so I didn't wear them. But Dad was too busy with the other lady to notice that I couldn't see.

I couldn't see the chalkboard, I couldn't see my friends, and I couldn't see where I was when the bus passed my stop late one night after a choir concert. All the other kids in the choir had gotten off at their respective stops while I sat alone on the bus—embarrassed because I couldn't see where I was and shy around kids I didn't know very well. I couldn't read the road signs, and nothing looked familiar.

It was getting dark, and the world seemed to close in on me and my blindness.

Finally, I saw a familiar building on the other side of town—our church's temple, lit with a comforting, brilliant white light. At the next stop, I exited the bus and nervously walked toward it, glancing back and forth in the shadows, afraid somebody might be hiding in the bushes and waiting to jump out and attack me. My heart was pounding. I couldn't see in the light, let alone in this haunting darkness.

I worked my way up the long, dark hill to the glowing white building with the tall spire on top. Although I wanted to run inside to safety, the sacred building was reserved for older people. I entered awkwardly and timidly approached a desk where a white-haired lady sat. "Can I please use the phone to call my dad?" I begged. "I got off on the wrong bus stop and now I'm lost."

I carefully dialed my home number on the heavy rotary phone and held my breath while I waited through several rings.

"Hello," Dad finally answered. Nearly in tears, I explained where I was and that I had missed my stop because I couldn't see and it was dark. I ended with, "Can you come and pick me up?"

After what seemed like hours, Dad came to my rescue. "Why didn't you get off earlier?" he scolded.

"I couldn't see," I countered.

Although Dad neglected his five young children while he sought a new wife in his pain and loneliness, he became my hero the day Mom died. And Mom became immortalized in my mind. On April 16, 1975, I wrote in my dairy:

> *Mom died today. I keep trying to tell myself that life is made up of the little things that happen in life not the big things—the smiles, the first time a baby walks or talks, the love little children have for one another. I have learned many things this day. My dad is the greatest dad ever. I love him with all my heart.*

To make sense of my new life, I tried to tell myself how blessed I was. I didn't see how much I needed Dad or how often Dad wasn't there. Mom shot herself, and then Dad, who was hardly home before, was gone even more. Work and church and the other lady took him away from his children. He relied on me to fill in the gaps.

I wrote about my pain in my bedroom, describing two parents who loved me:

Have you ever felt real loneliness,
With no one to tell your thoughts?
Have you ever felt really depressed,
Thinking of all your problems?
I have, I have.

At the conclusion of this song of pain, I resolutely proclaimed:

But then again have you ever had
A dad as swell as mine?
Or a mom who could understand
Just by looking in your eyes?
I have!

I tried to protect and take care of Dad by taking care of the kids, cleaning, and picking out headstones, but I didn't see that Dad, like Mom, was gone too. He left even before Mom did. He worked from morning until night to support the family—to create a lifestyle that would provide security and importance and love. That was all he knew how to do. He bought cars and motor homes and boats and vacations. And while he was chasing his dream, he lost the love of his life. He lost his high school sweetheart. And when he lost Mom, he lost his last flicker of light.

Dad had been abandoned himself when he was a child. When he was three years old—the oldest child of what were eventually seven children—he contracted rheumatic fever and spent the next three years at Primary Children's Hospital. His parents rarely visited him.

When Dad returned home from the hospital, his parents still weren't there for him. He was caught in an abusive environment devoid of love between his parents, and he was left to earn his own way by the time he was twelve. At fifteen, after an argument with Grandpa, my dad decided to run away. His dad grabbed him, stripped him naked, said that he could leave this world the way he entered it, and pushed Dad out the door.

So Dad worked. And after Mom died, he kept working. I had lost both my mom and my dad, but I couldn't see that through my glass mask.

❧ ❧

There were advantages to Dad being too busy with the other lady. I could stay out as late as I wanted to play night games, hang out with

Brad and Brad and my cousin Jackie in the motor home parked in our driveway, or toilet paper the house at the end of the street with my adventurous friends. I didn't have a curfew, and Dad was too busy with the other lady to notice when I came home.

Two weeks after meeting her, Dad announced that he would marry the other lady the day after my thirteenth birthday—exactly three months after he met her and five months, eighteen days after Mom shot herself.

We need a mom, I tried to tell myself. But this lady was cold and scary to me.

And she wasn't my mom. She couldn't bake bread or can fruit or plant gardens or comfort the sick. She couldn't even clean. Her house was a disastrous mess according to the twelve-year-old standards taught to me by my perfectionist mom. There were papers and books and old, dark furniture everywhere in that old witch's house, which had a creaky door and peeling paint and cobwebs up above the old, faded wallpaper. She caught my dad with one of those webs, I'm sure.

But she wouldn't catch me. She was scary.

And dark.

❧ ❧

Dad spent more and more time with the other lady—the lady I could never call *Mom*. She didn't come to our house much and we didn't go back to hers, but Dad was still determined to marry her.

The other lady, Jane, wasn't so sure about the arrangement, though. In fact, she tried to break off their engagement, but Dad didn't want to lose someone else. He did his best to convince Jane that she would have help with his five rowdy children. She reiterated that she would not take over as our mother.

Neighbors, relatives, friends, and even Marjean, the bishop's wife, wondered why Dad continued to pursue Jane when she was clearly so unmotherly. And they worried even more about the five of us kids when Jane told them that even though she wouldn't mother Dad's children, of course she would marry him—for sex and money. But still, Dad persisted.

One day, Dad came to me and asked, "Wendy, can you please go through Mom's clothes and decide which ones you'd like to keep and which ones you want to give away?"

I don't know if Dad just needed to make room for Jane's things or if he couldn't bear to have Mom's clothes hanging lifeless in the closet any longer—reminders of their life together that was no more. Regardless of why, I was ill equipped to carry the burden of choosing what to keep and what to toss.

How does a twelve-year-old know what piece of clothing or small memento might be meaningful to her years later when all she wants is to see her mom again, hear her laugh, touch her, feel her, tell her how much she loves her, and promise to be perfect if she won't go away? I wanted more than anything for God to return my mom to me.

How could I complete this daunting task? But I silently obeyed.

I knelt on the floor in Mom and Dad's bedroom and stared at the lifeless forms hanging limply from the cold metal hangers. I opened a purse and found a note in Mom's handwriting along with a gum wrapper. I got my gum chomping habit from Mom and tried to mimic her perfect handwriting. I watched Mom create beautiful masterpieces with her cursive letters as she helped me with my homework or wrote a short note to a neighbor or a letter to a friend. But I tossed aside the purse and with its contents.

I gasped a little when I pulled the first dress down and held it to my face. Although she had been gone for weeks, I smelled Mom—her perfume, her hair, her love and light and laughter. Mom was in and through and around that closet, but I couldn't see her. I couldn't touch or hear her. She was fading quickly from my memory, and my heart was heavy. I pushed aside the sadness and picked up another dress. I held it up to my chin and looked at myself in the mirror. *No, I won't wear this one,* I thought as I started a toss away pile on the bed. I held up dress after dress and blouse after blouse in the same fashion—deciding what to keep and what to toss, as though I had the ultimate power to rid the house of the ghosts that haunted it.

I tried on shoes and dresses and pants and blouses, but my twelve-year-old body was not quite right for Mom's clothes. Besides a couple of silky nightgowns and blouses I thought I might grow into, the rest ended up in the toss-away pile to clear away the memory.

I dismantled the closet that stood as evidence that Mom once lived. The closet still carried her favorite fragrances, Tabu and Chanel #5. I buried the evidence in a big garbage bag to be whisked away to the secondhand store. Maybe the pain, sadness, terror, loneliness, and heartache could be taken away to the secondhand store too.

19

A New Family Picture

My mind and body felt numb as I went through the motions of life. My mom's presence seemed a distant memory. I tried to reconcile my life without a mother and the life I wished God would grant me—one where Mom was restored and where my unbearable pain was washed away in her embrace as I told her all the things I wished I had said while she was still alive.

In this make-believe world, I could see her and touch her and smell her and hear her and love her, and she would love me, be proud of me, and stay with me. And she would live!

Instead, I was stuck between two worlds. I was stuck between the living and the dead. Ghosts continued to haunt my dreams at night. My world seemed anything but safe. I could no longer run to Mom to save me from the ghosts that had chased her, so I hid behind my glass mask. Piece by piece, Mom's memory was replaced by the other lady, who I could never call *Mom*. Life pushed forward, and I watched myself march to the drum of the rotating earth with my glass face and buried heart. When I was by myself, riding my bike in the rain, sitting next to Mom's grave, playing my guitar, or lying prostrate on my bedroom floor, I could be myself. I took the mask off and cried and cried and cried. And I asked why.

Why did Mom die? *I need to talk to someone about my problems. I need someone*, I had written. But I didn't have anyone. Mom was dead, and Dad was gone with the other lady. There was no one to protect me from the haunting ghosts. We were orphan children, and I was a twelve-year-old mom. I strained to carry the crushing weight.

❧ ❧

I put my glass face back on when Dad took all of us up to our cabin in our Sunday best for engagement pictures with the other lady and her eight-year-old daughter. I helped Dad get Annie and Drew ready, and I pulled on my angel dress for the visit to Mom's haven.

Our family had spent the past two summers with Mom at this mountain retreat, and we had returned to there for solace after Mom's death. Now we were tossing aside all of those memories to begin a new life with a new lady who didn't want to be our new mom.

It was difficult for the photographer to capture a picture of a happy family. Although I tried to keep my mask tightly in place, Cary wasn't about to fake happiness, and Drew and Marie wanted to run through the trees and grass of our big outdoor playground. Jane grabbed Annie on her lap and fought to keep the toddler from wriggling away.

Of course we acted like children—we *were* children. But Jane didn't like children. To us, her face was etched with hate and darkness. She was scary like the wicked witch in *The Wizard of Oz*. And it seemed she preferred to obliterate us like Dorothy and Toto so that she could keep the ruby slippers for herself.

Jane did love her own daughter, though. Sally was the same age and size as Marie but didn't have the same sense of adventure. She stoically obeyed everything her mother requested and seemed afraid not only of five rambunctious stepsiblings but also of her mother's disapproval. Dad was careful to dote on Sally even more than his own children to try to win her love at the same time he won Jane's. Sally connected almost instantly with Dad and lavished him with hugs and kisses in return. Dad eagerly accepted these, though he rarely hugged his own children. He never hugged me. In fact, Dad would take off his belt and threaten us if we were naughty or disobedient. He'd learned it from his dad.

I remembered one evening when I was about four and Cary was two. We were supposed to be sleeping, but it was light outside and other kids were riding bikes next to our bedroom window. Cary and I couldn't sleep, so we played. We laughed and giggled, and Cary played with his Tonka truck in bed.

Dad must have heard our delighted play. He stormed into the bedroom, belt in hand. I cowered in the corner of the top bunk and pretended to be asleep while Dad yelled at little Cary. Dad grabbed the truck away and snapped the belt between his hands. He threatened Cary with a whipping if he didn't go to sleep right then. I pulled the covers up and kept as quiet as I could to avoid his anger. I was nearly paralyzed with fear.

I still feared Dad's temper as I watched him love Jane and Sally. He didn't hug me, and I questioned his love. But he needed me. He didn't have Mom to take care of him anymore. He needed me to take care of the kids—to change diapers and babysit and fix meals and pick out headstones and toss away Mom's clothes. He needed me. That meant he loved me, didn't it?

Would he still need me once he replaced Mom with Jane?

Finally, the new picture for the engagement was snapped, the invitations were sent, and the old family pictures with Mom's bright smile were removed from the walls of our home in order to welcome the other lady into the house—the house where Mom had lived and died. Every picture of Mom was hidden away, as if erasing the memory of her life could hide the pain of her death.

20

A Broken Brain

I figured out pretty quickly that Jane didn't know how to take care of a houseful of kids. She came over every now and then for family home evening, but she remained stiff and distant. She didn't smile or play or laugh or have fun. And this lady was going to be our second mom? No way.

My cousin Karen told me years later that several months before her death—even before her cardiac arrest—Mom had fasted and prayed for guidance in choosing who my dad should marry when she died. After Mom's death, Dad saw Jane in a dream before he ever met her. Was this a sign from Mom that Jane was the one, or was it an ominous warning to stay away and protect the children from the darkness and pain of the other lady who hated children? Either way, Dad remained determined to take a second wife.

Jane even hated our friends. Until Jane came along, our house was open to the neighborhood—but afterwards, the door was closed to neighborhood intruders. These were our friends, who gave us our only sense of identity. Everything we knew had been ripped away, and Dad was trying to replace the hole with Jane. But Jane wouldn't replace anyone. She would not mother us.

We were pretty resourceful kids, and we weren't about to obey someone who demanded quiet and stillness and perfect obedience—especially when that someone didn't like us and glared at us like we were from Mars and corrected our English or our manners. Cary and

I both snuck out with our friends or invited them over when Dad and Jane were gone. One time Jane spent the entire day with us and met our friends. She became even more frantic. She didn't know how to tame us. She wanted out.

But Dad persisted. He wanted this marriage to work. He didn't want to lose another wife before their marriage even began. He was blinded by a dream and couldn't see the battle brewing between Jane and his five children. Jane was terrified to be in the same house with five kids she didn't love, and we were afraid of being hurt again. And things did not get better when Mrs. Smith, a few days before the wedding, announced that she would not continue on as nanny. Jane was ready to run away, but Dad persisted. And Jane agreed to stay—for sex and money.

❦ ❦

SUMMER 2012

"It's no secret that I don't like children," Jane said, her face etched with seventy-three years of anxiety, fear, anger, depression, and wear. Although she took medication for her bipolar disorder, she seemed to have more periods of depression and fewer of the alternating highs that helped her create art. Her life was defined by her paintings and awards, though she still remained unknown as an artist.

"I can't deal with children!" she declared again for emphasis. "They're so unpredictable."

I watched her from a distance. I felt outside of myself even though I sat next to her and my dad in their art- and antique-filled home. *Yes, it is no secret you don't like children,* I thought to myself. But I wasn't a child any more. I was a nearly fifty-year-old mom of four adult children and the grandmother of an adorable, high-energy, always-moving fourteen-month-old boy who was the light of my life.

"Jane," I said, "I'm worried about your brain. I'm worried about your memory."

Jane was in pretty good physical health. She faithfully walked four miles every day with my dad, followed by a weightlifting and stretching routine. But she had begun to show signs of cognitive decline, and I was worried about her. I shared my concerns with Dad at a Fourth of July family picnic thirty-seven years after Dad met Jane.

Sitting at the picnic table at Mom's haven, I had asked Jane if she had any applesauce at their house that I could get for my grandson.

"Is it all gone?" she answered.

"Jane, there wasn't any applesauce," I said, referring to the outdoor banquet table filled with an array of potluck surprises. Dad had purchased the property next to Mom's cabin and now lived with Jane in a new house at the top of the hill.

"Yes, I'm sure there was applesauce," Jane said slowly, her eyebrows furrowed. "I just ate some."

"No, I don't think so. There wasn't any applesauce. Do you mean the potato salad?"

"There's not any applesauce?" Jane questioned. "I'm sure I just ate some," she said, confusion on her face.

When I shook my head again, Jane said, "Hmm. I'll go up to the house and see if we have any more."

Shortly, she returned with a plate of applesauce and cottage cheese for our baby boy. She walked slowly down the dirt road that led from the house to the cabin, bundled in several layers. Her head and face were covered by a black scarf blowing softly behind her. Although it was summertime, Jane dressed like most people do in the middle of winter. She was always cold, due in part to her skeletal, one-hundred-five-pound, five-foot-seven-inch frame. She didn't think she was too thin, however, and had just completed a several-day lemon juice fast as a treatment to reduce her back pain. I was worried because she would go off her medication when she fasted. She seemed more disengaged at family events. Dad was worried about how thin she was, but he couldn't get her to eat much. And he was even more worried when I told him about her confusion over the applesauce. I suggested that a doctor visit would be a good idea.

"Can you come up to the house and talk to Jane?" Dad asked. Evidently, she had displayed prior episodes of confusion and forgetfulness, and she wasn't convinced that she needed help—or even a more substantial diet.

As we talked in the living room, it was clear that Dad loved Jane. He was aware of her confusion with the applesauce, but he spoke of her with concern and tenderness. He spoke of their mission in life to help the family—a kind of redemption for their shortcomings years earlier when they didn't know how to bandage our wounds. Though retired, they offered financial help—sometimes until it hurt. They were blessing the lives of their children and grandchildren with music lessons, college tuition, and mission funds.

"It's been difficult for all of us," Dad said. "We'll continue to do as much as we can to help our children and grandchildren." He and Jane never missed plays, choir concerts, ball games, or graduations. In family home evening, Dad now freely shared his tears as he expressed his love and faith. "We were all hurt by the awful tragedy of Mom's death, but with patience and love, I know we can overcome our problems."

And there were many.

One time, while picking apples, Dad and Jane spoke briefly to me about Cary and Drew, young men who needed financial support long after other young men were able to begin their families. Dad was always there to lend them money and provide jobs for them. Dad hoped to give them both an opportunity to learn his trade so they could be financially independent after he died. When Dad wondered why Cary and Drew struggled so much in life, I answered, "Because they lost their mom."

"And I couldn't do it," Jane said sadly. "I couldn't be their mom."

"No. You were sick," Dad agreed with tenderness and concern in his voice.

"I know I wasn't able to cope," Jane said. "It's hard to understand this sickness."

I was struggling to understand this kind of sickness in a person myself, and I now began to wonder if Mom had also been sick. My PhD nurse cousin suspected that Mom had also suffered from a form of bipolar disorder. She said that at times Mom had an unmatched energy and zest for life—walking and talking faster than anyone else, accomplishing more than humanly possible—and at other times a severe lethargy that made it impossible for her to get out of bed. I remember only Mom's highs until her cardiac arrest—and then she could hardly move. Looking at pictures, though, I see a hint of sadness in her eyes beneath her captivating smile. Other cousins suspected she might have had postpartum depression after giving birth to Drew and again after Annie was born.

After her cardiac arrest, Mom was determined to die.

"Linda! Give me that gun!" Dad had yelled one night. As he described in his memoir, Dad slapped Mom's face, trying to jolt her from her determination. He'd found Mom shooting bags of wheat in the storage room and had grabbed the hunting rifle from her. Dad dismantled the gun and hid it in the storage room behind bags of flour and wheat and canned honey and stashed the bullets and bolt on another shelf where Mom couldn't find them.

Aunt Grace described sharing a hospital room with a woman who had a psychiatric condition. When Mom came to visit, Grace encouraged Mom to go see Dr. Robert Crist, a psychiatrist. "I think he could help you, Linda," she said.

Mom stubbornly assured Grace that she could treat herself with herbs and natural remedies and that she didn't need a psychiatrist. Grace remained concerned about her mental state, though—Mom shared thoughts of death and described to her sisters how she would end her life. She found the dismantled gun in the storage room and replaced the bullets and bolt. "You know how Dick shot himself," Mom said to Grace, speaking of their brother who had tried to end his life by drinking Drano and shooting himself in the stomach. "I'm going to do that too," she said, and she confessed practicing with the rifle.

Dick survived. Mom lay dead in a pool of blood.

❧ ❧

As Dad and Jane continued talking with me that evening in the living room, I expressed my concerns to Jane. "Jane, I'm worried about your memory," I said again. "There wasn't any applesauce on the table today."

"I know I ate some applesauce," Jane said, looking at Dad across the room for encouragement and answers. "When did I eat applesauce?"

"Jane, it might be good to get your brain tested," I said. Dad agreed that she should see a doctor. "You need to eat better to feed your brain."

"Well . . . maybe I should get help," Jane said with difficulty. Her mouth seemed dry, and her lips stuck to her teeth because of her long fast. "I'm just in so much pain. When I fast, the inflammation goes away. I feel so good when I don't eat. Sometimes I think I would be fine if I never ate."

"But Jane, you need to nourish your brain. And you can't do that with just lemon juice," I explained. "You need some good protein and carbohydrates and healthy fats."

"I try to get her to eat," Dad said to me. "We eat chicken a couple of times a week. And some fish."

Dad was clearly worried about her health and her brain. I watched as Dad and Jane bantered back and forth, Dad reinforcing the need to stop fasting and see a doctor. Jane tried to remember why she thought she had just eaten applesauce.

Jane was suffering from emotional incompetency and confusion about the applesauce, and she was probably misconnecting many other events. Her memory was beginning to fail her. Though she was careful to take her medication, she still struggled with an illness that was almost impossible to understand.

But despite Jane's difficulties, she expressed her gratitude that someone in the family cared. "Thank you, Wendy, for caring. It's so nice to have someone care. I know I wasn't able to cope with the family . . . and I'm sorry." Jane continued to express her thanks, adding that she felt like no one cared that she was an artist. "I don't think I'm going to paint anymore."

"Oh, Jane," Dad said, "You have to keep painting."

In that moment, I began to feel compassion for Jane—the lady I could never call *Mom*. As I watched her, I felt her sadness and her longing for importance, her desire to make a mark on the world. And yet she felt like no one cared. And if no one cared about her paintings or her contributions to the family, then what was her life for? We all desire to be important to someone. We all desire to make a mark on this earthly existence. We all desire to leave a legacy.

I sensed her tremendous heaviness and realized how difficult it was for Jane to feel love. Her mental illness had limited her ability to feel happiness and joy and light and love. And I felt sad for her.

Dad loved Jane. Despite her limitations, she had added many blessings to his life, and he didn't want to lose her.

"Where did we have applesauce?" Jane asked again. "I know I just ate applesauce." After talking through the last couple of days with Dad, Jane finally remembered that she had eaten applesauce the day before at her sister's.

"It feels like I just ate applesauce," Jane insisted. "When you're as old as I am, a day feels like five minutes. Life goes faster the older you get. A friend of mine just died at eighty-six," she said. "That's only thirteen more years for me. That's not enough time. It's just a flash."

Jane had suffered from mental illness her whole life, but she *chose* to live. Now Dad and Jane were looking at the end of their lives, and I watched them love each other. And I said to myself, *Maybe Jane really was the other lady Mom chose for Dad. Through all the heartache, fear, anger, depression, fights, running, and hiding—through all the mental illness, they love each other. Maybe she really was the one.*

And then I heard Mom say, *Wendy, you need to take care of her. You need to love her.*

And I prayed I could.

21

Birthdays Alone

Friday, October 3, 1975, was my thirteenth birthday. Since I didn't have a mom, and since Dad was getting married the next morning, he asked a friend of Jane's—a lady I had never met—to chaperone my sleepover birthday party at our cabin, Mom's heavenly retreat.

All of my girlfriends from church came with their sleeping bags and boxes of treats. The chaperone of the party was not a member of our ward. Even though she didn't know any of us, she did her best to support our fun. She let us stay up late and tell ghost stories and gossip about the boys we liked and the girls we were jealous of. But she wasn't Mom. My friends talked about their periods, but I hadn't experienced one yet, so I remained silent, uncomfortable with all the openness. I didn't have a mom to guide me through that next phase of life. I was turning thirteen alone. I was a teenager alone. All grown-up—but stuck at twelve.

While the chaperone slept in Mom's bedroom, we lined the family room with our sleeping bags and skillfully changed into our pajamas inside the tiny tubes. I slept next to the fireplace and pushed aside thoughts of Mom or ghosts peering through the blackened windows that opened to the dark night.

It had been six months since Mom died, and my shell was nearly impenetrable. I was worried about Dad's marriage to Jane the next morning, but I was tough. Jane was determined to make her wedding dress of simple white eyelet lace and a big, floppy white hat. She had to unpick the dress several times, but eventually, she pieced it together.

We girls were to be dressed in pink pioneer dresses with white aprons and white pioneer bonnets. My preteen brain couldn't comprehend how Dad could toss aside my mom and fall in love with a second wife, and my heart was covered tightly with rocks and dirt, ensuring I would never love Jane.

After breakfast the next morning, while Dad and Jane were saying their wedding vows, I hiked along the riverbed behind the cabin with my friends and collected flowers and weeds for the tiny vases the chaperone had brought for each girl.

Mom loved dried flower arrangements. She taught me how to place clipped flowers in a shoebox and carefully pour fine sand over the flowers in order to suck out all the water. To preserve a likeness of life, of beauty that once was, you had to suck all the life out of the flower. Then, though dead, the flower's beauty remained.

But this beauty was easily destroyed. The dead and dried flowers crumbled beneath even the lightest of touch. But if protected by glass, the flowers remained whole. Masterful arrangements hung on our living room wall—a last reminder of the beauty buried beneath layers of cold rocks and earth like her pictures lay buried in a cardboard box in the ghost-haunted basement.

I was alone on my birthday the year before, too. Two days before I turned twelve, Mom nearly died of her cardiac arrest. Grandpa had volunteered to let Mom stay at his home in Salt Lake City until she regained enough strength to return to us. The afternoon of my twelfth birthday, my cousin Karen drove me to Grandpa's house to visit Mom. As we pulled up on the dusty lane winding past the hogs and horses and rabbits that Grandpa raised for food and fun, I saw Mom lying in a recliner outside in the sunshine, still in her nightgown and wrapped in a blanket.

Too weak to move, Mom greeted me with half a smile as I stood over her. I didn't know what to say. I was afraid of losing her. I didn't realize I already had. She was just a shadow of her earlier self—fragile, weak, and distant. She couldn't care for me any longer, so I did my best to care for her.

I felt lost. Mom had always made birthdays special. She made fancy cakes and hosted parties with lots of friends and presents and games. That year, though, I was afraid my mom would die.

And she did.

The last birthday gift Mom ever gave me was a pine jewelry box from Yellowstone. My own children used it year after year in our family Christmas pageants to carry gifts of gold, frankincense, and myrrh to the Christ child.

She also gave me my first set of scriptures engraved with my name. From the recliner, Mom encouraged me to read them in order to draw closer to Heavenly Father and Jesus Christ. I promised I would.

A few years later, I finally finished those scriptures, underlining verse after verse that proclaimed God's goodness and testified of Jesus Christ, who came to Earth to show us the way and died so that we could live again. I read of Jesus's love for me. I learned that He took upon Himself my sins so that if I repented, I could be made whole and return to live with Him again in heaven.

I read the scriptures Mom gave me many times, and I read them to my children. I taught my children about Jesus's love for them, and I prayed that I could someday feel that love too. I thought to myself, *If I could feel that love, maybe Jesus would remove the bandages around my heart and clean out the dirt and rocks and buried pain.* Maybe then my heart could heal.

22

The Stain

Oh my gosh, I gasped to myself. *What's all this blood?* My heart raced, and my palms dripped with anxiety. I sat, horrified, on the toilet in the bathroom where Mom had shot herself. I wiped again, staining the white toilet paper red-brown. I breathed heavily, frozen on the toilet, not knowing what to do. I wiped again. More blood.

This must be the period that all my friends have talked about, I thought. *Now what?*

A first period can be traumatic under the best of circumstances, but this was the worst of circumstances. There I was, sitting alone in a bathroom where Mom lay dead in a pool of blood just a few months before—a bathroom haunted with blood splatters and ghosts and weapons. And I sat on the toilet, trapped in this space by blood—my blood.

And I could tell no one. I was completely alone.

I sat there for several more minutes wondering what to do. I finally shuffled my way across the floor to the bottom drawer of the linen cupboard at the opposite end of the bathroom, my underwear at my ankles. I used toilet paper as a bandage to prevent the blood from splattering on the floor that had been scoured clean after Mom died.

I opened the bottom drawer and found a half-used box of Mom's tampons. I shuffled back to the toilet, box in hand. I pulled out the instructions and reviewed the pictures that detailed how to insert it. They made me uncomfortable; I felt like I was looking at pornography, though I'd never seen any before. I opened the wrapper and was confused by the telescoping cardboard. After examining the contents, I tried to insert one end inside me to stop the flow of blood. Before I had advanced the tampon, the bottom half fell off, nearly landing in the toilet. Now I had to try to put the dirty tampon back together and start over. I was flustered and nearly frantic by this point.

Needless to say, I was unprepared to be sitting alone in the bathroom, teaching myself how to insert my first tampon. The cardboard applicator was stiff and dry and scratchy, and I was afraid I might put it too far in. If I did, how would I get it out?

And I had to get ready for school. But how could I go to school with something up inside me? I was supposed to be excited that I was growing up. Some of my friends' moms even took them out to eat or bought them a new outfit to celebrate this step to young womanhood. But I didn't feel like celebrating. Having something up inside of me made me feel dirty and embarrassed and ashamed and afraid and alone and sick to my stomach. I felt like I had when I'd been raped by a male teenage babysitter a few years earlier while the rest of my siblings played outside my bedroom door. I wanted to hide then too, or throw up or run away.

I wanted my mom.

But I didn't want my mom to see how bad I was. I didn't want my mom to know I had lied to her. When I was about ten years old, Mom told me about a boy hurting my little sister's private parts. Mom asked, "Has anything like that ever happened to you?" I looked straight at Mom, shook my head, and said, "No." Immediately, my face felt red-hot, and I'd thought I might pass out from the weight of the guilt. But I stood firm and resolutely repeated, "No." I lied to her about my hurt, pain, guilt, and shame.

And now I could hide no longer. She could see all my mistakes—mistakes that would surely thrust me down to hell.

When I went to Europe the next summer with several of my girl-friends—a trip my mom was excited for me to take with my junior-high French class—Mom could surely see when I passionately kissed a boy I thought I loved. Mom could see when I froze from fear and didn't say no to a boy who tried to put his hand up my shirt. Mom could see, and God would punish.

I was alone in guilt and shame that stemmed from early childhood abuse. I tried to distance myself from the darkness by reading scriptures, going to church, and trying to be perfect in every other way. But I was certain that hell would be my final resting place. And then I would never see Mom even though Mom could see me.

I dated and danced and fell in and out of love with boyfriend after boyfriend, trying to fill the empty space where Mom had shot me. I wrote love poems to these boys that I never shared with them:

> Am I seeing things when you sit near me?
> Am I hearing things when you say, "I love you"?
> Am I dreaming when you kiss me?
> Are we really in love, or is it just a fantasy?
> How can I be sure? Please tell me!

I wrote songs and dreamed dreams and waited for the perfect man, who would take me away from the buried pain. All the while, I kept my glass face firmly in place and smiled and laughed and pretended. At night, when I was alone by my bed, I removed the glass face and prayed and pleaded with God to forgive me. I prayed to be spared from hell.

⚜ ⚜

SUMMER 1977

"Annie, get off the chair!" I commanded. "You don't need to sit there!"

"Two!" Jane countered, her face taut with anger as she pointed her long, wicked finger at Annie.

Three-year-old Annie had been sequestered on a hard chair in time-out for playing "nasty" with a neighbor boy, who touched her private parts. I was trying to protect my baby sister from Jane, who didn't know the first thing about mothering and had told Annie how babies were made.

Annie looked from me to Jane and back to me, confused about whom to obey. Sensing my approval, she defiantly left the chair. Jane immediately grabbed her and slammed her back on the chair.

"Three!" Jane shouted.

"You don't put a three-year-old in time-out for three hours!" I screamed at the top of my lungs, unaware that the counting meant minutes.

I was out of control. I hated this lady. She was a terrible mother, and I told her so.

"You are not going to put my baby sister in time-out for three hours! That's not how you teach a child!" I shouted again.

"Go, Annie, go!" I encouraged.

"Don't you dare leave that chair!" demanded Jane.

Jane had no business pretending to mother us. She spanked Marie when time-out didn't work, and her long, sharp fingernails grabbed at Marie's skin. One time they drew blood. Sally tried to quiet Marie's muffled sobs then. "Shh! Don't let her hear you. She'll just hurt you more," Sally whispered as she placed cold compresses on Marie's welts.

Dad ignored my accusations when I told him of Jane's abuse. I was powerless to protect my little sisters.

Aside from Sally, Drew was Jane's favorite. Drew avoided trouble with his cute dimpled smile, his freckled face, and his mischievous teasing. Cary and I were nearly as big as Jane was, so she hid from us instead of punishing us. And we hid from her as much as possible, staying out late with friends or roaming the streets. Cary drank and partied. I hung around with boys and participated in as many school activities as I could. We stayed away from Jane.

But Annie and Marie were too young to protect themselves. And in the end, I couldn't protect them either. There was no one to protect any of us. Not from sin, not from abuse, and not from the watchful eye of my dead mom. I was all alone—alone with my sins, that dark stain that started when I was raped and followed me throughout my life, that made me feel dirty with the "sin" of having a period or kissing a boy. I tried to be the big sister I was supposed to be, to save my siblings from Jane, but I couldn't—not when I was so imperfect. And I knew my perfect mom could see it all.

23

My Perfect Mom

Dad was the self-appointed family photographer. At every family event, Dad carried his old Kodak camera on one shoulder and his sixteen-millimeter movie camera on the other, recording the intimate details of his life—or rather the lives of those closest to him.

As young children, we were delighted to curl up in our pajamas with our pillows and blankets lined up on the floor of our basement family room and applaud our stardom in Dad's home movies, which he projected on the big white screen at the other end of the room. We gained a sense of self as we fondly remembered annual family vacations, birthday parties, and camping trips. We cemented lifelong traditions as we viewed these masterpieces, and we enthusiastically rediscovered favorite birthday cakes, Easter baskets, and Halloween costumes immortalized in these silent films.

Under my blanket, I watched myself instantly grow from a bright, toddling one-year-old to an energetic four-year-old on a magical Christmas morning with my first easy-bake oven. I knew Santa was real, and I had the home movie to prove it.

As a young girl, I looked just for me—catching a glimpse of a rosy-cheeked girl bundled in a slippery snowsuit, racing down an icy hill on her red Flexible Flyer sled or an embarrassed, pigeon-toed kindergartner who had to summon enough courage to hold hands with a boy for the first time ever when she danced at the May Day festival. But when Dad dusted off the movie projector for a family-night activity a few years after Mom died, I watched instead for my baby sister. I noted in my journal how fast Annie had grown up and how I longed to hold her little self in my arms just one more time.

Years later, sitting next to my own daughter, Becca, I studied my mom. *She holds her hand just like I do, with her elbow on the kitchen table and her hand hanging limp in the air like it's not even attached*, I thought to myself with a smile,

I watched reel after reel as if for the first time, trying to learn who my mom was. She flitted around with light and energy like a hummingbird drinking sweet nectar from the butterfly bush, then disappearing at light speed and daring you to find her. The rest of the family had to run to keep up.

I smiled when I watched Mom hold me as an infant and spoon baby food down my dimpled face. "What is she doing feeding solids to a two-month-old?" I gasped to Becca. "That must have been the start of my food obsession!" I laughed.

I watched, horrified, as Dad tossed this same dark-haired two-month-old over Mom's big stuffed dog and balanced me there like a rag doll while Mom kept the camera rolling to capture my first Christmas.

When Mom placed a coconut-covered cake shaped like an elephant on my highchair tray to celebrate my first birthday, she turned and shared her radiant smile with the camera. Mom had replaced her long, strawberry-blond hair with a short, no-frills sixties-style bob and had carefully pulled my hair into a pony tail on top of my head, accenting it with a frilly bow. By this time, thick blond curls reached nearly to my shoulders.

Though only five-foot-two, Mom filled the screen with life. Dad loved taking pictures of his high school sweetheart. He loved capturing her radiant smile and beauty. Dad loved Mom!

The home movies reminded me of things the cameras hadn't captured—stories that I'd heard from the family when I was little as well as stories I read about later in Dad's memoir. Dad didn't immediately fall in love with Mom when he first met her in their church youth group. She was twelve and he was fifteen. Dad's father was the scoutmaster and the president of the young men's group. According to Dad, Grandpa's natural charisma attracted many of the youth to him. A girls' youth leader in the same congregation described Grandpa as a flirt with the young women. Grandpa stayed late after each activity and talked with the girls and their leaders. He teased them and socialized with them and danced with them instead of going home to his own wife.

The youth thought Grandpa was great, but some of the mothers were concerned about their daughters and asked the church to replace him. No change was made. Grandpa continued in his role as scoutmaster, and he continued flirting.

Like many of the other young girls, Mom thought Grandpa was the best. She even wrote, as a thirteen-year-old, in her journal about Grandpa and the fun they had at the youth activities.

The first time Dad paid any attention to Mom, she was with some friends at his home. Dad wrote:

> It must have been on a Saturday morning in the late spring or early summer when I went out into the shed where my dad was butchering and pelting the rabbits. I no sooner rounded the corner and went into the shed than I saw these three girls giggling and having fun as my father went about his work.
>
> There was Linda in her white, long-sleeved blouse with the sleeves rolled up and her jeans rolled up to her calf. She seemed to be having a great time. She would take the eyeball of a rabbit and squeeze it between her fingers as if squashing a grape. I thought this was unusual for a girl to be doing. Her blonde ponytail swung from side to side as she tried to intimidate her friends.

It was several more months before Dad asked Mom to a church dance. Mom said yes, and the love story began.

Mom had many friends, both girls and boys, and she wasn't afraid to whip those friends on the ball field. She loved all sports—baseball, basketball, volleyball, ice skating, horseback riding—and she excelled athletically.

In addition to the stories, I had other records of my mom. Mom's *Book of Remembrance* and *Treasures of Truth* portfolios contained cards, letters, and even progress reports, which I devoured. Mom did well enough academically, earning mostly A's and B's and an occasional C on her report card. She especially liked socializing with her friends at school. One teacher in junior high commented on her report card, "Linda needs to talk less and work harder in class." Another wrote, "Linda does a lot of unnecessary talking in class. She would do better work if she would concentrate on her own work."

After a school year of weekend dates and a first Christmas together, Mom wrote in Dad's first high-school yearbook:

Hi Wally (Peach) s.w.a.k. You are a real swell kid and I have enjoyed knowing you for the last eight months. You are very cute and have a personality that anyone would like . . . I like your poetry you write. You really have a natural talent for it. I do believe I have a couple of boy friends, but you are my top "man."

In addition to all this, I had the memories of the people who grew up with Mom. Even though Mom bragged to Dad about her other boyfriends, her older sister Grace said that the only one Mom could talk about to her was Dad. "Theirs was truly a Cinderella story," Grace said. "Your dad was always at our home. He was just one of the family."

Mom worried about Dad's heavy load and encouraged him to balance his schoolwork with his various after-school jobs. And although she was two years Dad's junior, Mom confidently bossed him around—and Dad obeyed.

When Dad wasn't working or at school, he was at Mom's house, enjoying Grandma Eva's home cooked meals. Mom's home was full of love and respect and happiness. Dad found respite in Mom's home, away from the fighting and yelling and filth of his dysfunctional family.

Grandma Eva worked from dawn until dusk planting and harvesting and cleaning and cooking and canning, stocking her cellar shelves with hundreds of bottles of homemade jams and jellies and canned fruits and vegetables. Grandma taught her children the law of the harvest despite their meager means. During one of his many visits, Dad captured a sunny, fourteen-year-old Linda canning pears in Grandma Eva's small, sterile kitchen on his old black-and-white camera.

Mom's home was filled with love and harmony, order, and hard work. Dad's dirty, disorderly home echoed the shrill screeching of a mother trying to command seven young children or get attention from an abusive husband. My dad had a battered mother. Grandma once described to me a husband—my grandpa—who raped and beat and belittled her.

And cheated on her.

The teenage girl who would be my mom recounted to her sisters many stories of explosive fights between Dad's parents. Dad escaped the chaos and found shelter at Grandma Eva's as often as possible. He accompanied Mom to the many activities Mom's large family hosted. They came together for picnics, camping trips, holiday celebrations, and birthdays. The family grew as, one by one, all of Mom's eight older siblings got married and started their own families. Mom and Dad happily babysat these nieces and nephews, rehearsing married life at Mom's sisters' homes.

Mom and Dad's love story continued through Mom's junior high and high school years—complete with all the ups and downs and jealousies and drama of an adolescent love life. At times they dated exclusively; at other times they reluctantly decided they should date others too. While Mom was in her last two years of high school, Dad spent time in the army. In her letters to him, Mom kept Dad apprised of the occasional dates she went on and told him with whom she spent time, but she assured Dad that these other boys meant nothing to her and avowed her never-ending love for Dad.

Dad was the oldest of seven children, and Mom was the youngest of nine. Although Mom described their life in a tiny home with a big garden as "meager" (she even recalled sleeping on a trunk as a little girl), Grandpa Rowley spoiled his youngest daughter. Aunt Grace described a playful little sister excited to see her dad return home from work with half his ham sandwich still in his lunch pail. Grandpa Rowley would invariably give it to his little girl. Mom danced to life with an innocent naiveté, a youngest daughter who had her dad wrapped around her finger.

Mom wrote a letter to her father while on one of the many trips we took back east to visit my dad's parents. On June 8, 1969, she wrote:

> *You know, Dad, I was telling everyone the other day about when I got burned and how you saved my life, and I thought of how many times I have been grateful to you for what you did and the fact that I have never in all these years expressed to you the gratitude and love I have for you. It was a very brave thing you did, and I will always be grateful to you for it. It isn't every father that could have done that. So since I have never been one for being able to express myself, I thought I would tell you in a letter. Thanks, Dad, for saving my life and for always being an example for me to look up to and be proud of.*
>
> *I have always thought that if I could just teach my kids to have half the respect and love for me and their dad as we do for you and mom that I could say I was a pretty successful parent. I can't help but think I am failing miserably. I only hope I am wrong.*

When I read this letter for the first time, I wanted to shout at her. "Mom, you weren't failing miserably! I love you. I miss you! I thought you could do no wrong. I wanted to be just like you—outgoing and positive and energetic and kind and compassionate and full of life. I wanted to bake bread and sprout sprouts and have babies and be perfect, just like I knew you were! I wanted you to hold me and love me."

I wanted so desperately to feel her love. But instead, I buried my heart with rocks and put on a glass face.

Mom finished her letter to her dad:

> *Always know that I love you and appreciate all that you have done for me—at least all that I know about. There is so much that I am not even aware of. Better close now. See you in a few days.*
> *Your baby girl,*
> *Linda (Pin-head).*

Grandpa Rowley never saw her letter. We returned from that vacation a few hours after he died. As an adult, reading this letter for the first time, I shared Mom's sadness and loss. I'm certain that Mom's twenty-five-year-old heart broke as she buried her dad next to her mom, who had died eight years earlier. I'm sure there were many other things left unsaid—words she wished she had spoken before her dad took his last breath.

And though Mom's written words were captured in a card to her dad and her smile was captured on a silent film, Mom's final "I love you" to her husband and her children remained unspoken because she pulled the trigger.

24

The Secret

"Mom, why is Great-grandpa in all the home movies with your mom?" Becca asked as I pored over the home movie DVDs my dad had given me for Christmas a few years earlier.

John had led me on a painful journey of discovery that I hoped would someday lead to peace. He encouraged me to talk to as many people as I dared about Mom. The goal was to eventually desensitize myself to the trauma of her death. I scoured my home for anything I could find about my mom—pictures, notes, baby books—and I began telling people about her life and death. But I didn't want to tell anyone about Grandpa.

My earliest recollection of my dad's dad is my earliest recollection of my life. I was two years old, riding in our old, red, 1959 Ford pickup truck with my mom. My little brother Cary was strapped in his infant seat. I leaned against the creaky door, and the door latch gave way. I tumbled out onto the hard pavement below. It was dark outside, and a stream of headlights whizzed by. I was frightened and alone for harrowing minutes before my frantic mom could stop and rescue me. She scooped me off the pavement and rushed me to Grandpa's house for emergency treatment. Grandpa placed me on his bed and picked the gravel from my bleeding hands and knees. After bandaging my wounds, he let me jump on his bed and gave me love, kisses, and candies.

Grandpa, it seemed, was always there, and he was a big part of my life. He was responsible for my extensive dental work; he always had a sugary treat in his pocket ready to share with me or my siblings.

Grandpa was there for Christmas celebrations, birthdays, and camping trips. He often visited our home in the evenings when Dad worked late or attended his church leadership meetings. When Grandpa worked in Iowa and Illinois for a few years, Mom and Dad took us to visit him and Grandma back east.

On one of our many trips there, I proudly sat next to Grandma as we drove, just the two of us, the hundreds of miles from Utah to Illinois—blazing a trail the rest of the family would follow a few days later. I was five or six years old.

Grandma was a sturdy lady with short, wavy black hair, baby-blue eyes set in a stern face, and false teeth she removed whenever she told a scary story. I loved Grandma, but I was afraid of her too. I was her oldest grandchild, and she spoiled me with prizes, homemade cookies, birthday presents, and a trip by myself across the United States.

We must have sung "Ninety-Nine Bottles of Beer on the Wall" a million times as we made our way through golden corn fields, rolling hills, and flat plains to a fort somewhere in Nebraska or South Dakota, where we stopped and discovered the Indians of the Wild West. We smiled for a picture in the souvenir paper at the old-time printing press and watched a shiny penny tumble to its death and exit a red machine as a flattened landscape picture. After learning all we could about the cowboys and Indians of days long past, we continued our journey across the plains. For as long as the trek seemed to a young girl, it felt as though we had traveled by covered wagon.

At last, our journey was complete and we arrived at Grandma and Grandpa's home in Romeoville, Illinois.

In the days before the rest of the family arrived, I had fun helping Grandma bake cookies with recipes she made up. She was an expert, and she showed me how to measure salt, flour, sugar, and baking powder with just her hands. She didn't use measuring spoons or measuring cups; she merely used her experience. A teaspoon was about the size of a dime in the palm of her hand, and a tablespoon about the size of a quarter. She scooped out cups full of fluffy flour in her open hand and tossed the white, dusty bombs into a big mixing bowl to which she added the final, yummy ingredients—chocolate chips and nuts or raisins. Every batch tasted different, and yet every batch was uniquely Grandma.

Grandma was the President of our church's Relief Society women's organization in Romeoville. She oversaw all the adult women in her congregation and made sure their temporal and spiritual needs were met. She always had extra food to take to the less fortunate and would have given the shirt off her back if someone else had needed it. She died penniless because she had given away everything she owned.

Grandma seemed like two different people—at times a generous saint and at other times an impatient, accusatory, and out-of-control marshal who blasted her children, grandchildren, husband, and even her friends for the slightest infractions. If she couldn't find a certain necklace or a dollar bill she had set on the counter, she was certain that her grandchildren were thieves who had stolen from her. And she would punish accordingly.

Thankfully, I never received Grandma's punishment, but while I stayed with her in Romeoville, I watched her tie up two of my younger cousins—her oldest daughter's girls. Grandma angrily sat these girls on kitchen chairs on the back deck and tied them to the chairs with towels. Their hands were behind their backs so they couldn't move. I watched the abuse, silent and afraid and guilty as I walked free while my young cousins begged to be loosed.

I also stayed silent one time when Grandma yelled uncontrollably at Grandpa. He coolly countered, "Florence, shut up or I'm going to hit you."

When Grandma continued her ranting, Grandpa continued his threats. "Shut up, I said! What do you want? Do you *want* me to hit you?"

Finally, when Grandpa had had enough of Grandma's shrieking, he slapped her across the face. If that didn't shut her up, he punched her. I even saw him hit her with a two-by-four.

But he never hit me.

And I loved him.

Grandpa, at least to me, was like Bert from *Mary Poppins*—playful, energetic, and fun. My dad loved his little family, but he was like Mr. Banks—stiff and rigid and driven by his sense of duty to provide for his family.

Grandpa loved little children, and they loved him. When he was declining from Alzheimer's, I took my four young children to visit their great-grandpa. Although Grandpa could only speak in little snippets—fragments of thoughts embedded in a puzzle of incoherent phrases—he did remember that Becca was born prematurely. He said to her, "We almost lost you." After another random thought, he talked about the nursery class he and his second wife taught at church. He said, "All the little children run to me."

After several more unconnected strands of memory, he looked again at Becca and said sadly, "You used to run to me too." Children were definitely the sunshine in Grandpa's life, and as his memory faded, he sought to recapture that light.

Grandpa was proud of his grandchildren. Where my dad was uncomfortable hugging or teasing or playing with us—and was working all the time—Grandpa was there to fill in the gap. He taught us to fish and explore and swing and play. He wiped away our tears and bandaged our owies.

Grandpa was funny and smart. In fact, he was a genius. Grandpa showed off his math expertise by using only his head to race my dad on his business calculator to figure out complex math problems. Grandpa always won.

Grandpa loved airplanes and had his pilot license. On one of our trips back east, Grandpa took us to the airport control tower to watch the planes land. Then he took us high above the city in a small plane. He scared us with dips and climbs and taught us about all the controls. I adored Grandpa.

And Grandpa loved Mom. As I watched the silent home movies with Becca, I understood even more just how big a part of Mom's life Grandpa was. But I hid the truth from my daughter. How could I talk about Grandpa and Mom's relationship without tarnishing the beautiful, perfect person I knew as my Mom?

When I was fourteen, I read my mom's diary. I wrote in my own journal:

> Oh, by the way, I found my mom's diary from when she was my age, and she was as corny as I am.

My fourteen-year-old journal was full of romances, crushes, fantasies, and jealousies. I started a diet every other day in order to win some boy or another. I wrote about the adventures of sneaking out with my best girlfriend and about our plans to go to Tampa, Florida, to reconnect with the long-lost loves we met in Europe.

My mom's diary resonated with me. She too described the boys she madly loved and the fun she had with her girlfriends. Her diary has since been lost, but I read it a second time in my early twenties, and I was struck by Mom's description of her crush on Grandpa.

While Grandpa was the scoutmaster in their church, he helped each of his five sons and countless other young men earn their Eagle awards. For his own scouting efforts, Grandpa received every single merit badge offered and eventually received the Silver Beaver award as a distinguished leader.

With her girlfriends, Mom routinely attended the same weekly youth activities that Grandpa and Dad attended. In her diary, Mom talked about Grandpa for several pages. Although Aunt Grace had described a little sister madly in love with Dad, Mom wasn't shy about professing her adoration for the man whose namesake she would marry five years later.

All the memories, accounts, and diary entries swirled in my mind as I watched the home movies with my daughter. I made an uncomfortable excuse for Grandpa's presence—at the same time observing the almost adulterous way my old, round Grandpa lay on the boat in his bathing suit, soaking up the sun next to my swimsuit-clad nineteen- or twenty-year-old mom while my dad captured the moment for all time with his movie camera.

Why did Dad allow Grandpa on this trip in the first place? I thought to myself. Grandpa was the only other person to accompany Mom and Dad on what should have been a romantic getaway for newlyweds. Surely Dad must have been uncomfortable with the advances his own father made toward his wife. *What power did Grandpa have over Dad? Or did Dad just not want to see it?*

I watched film after film of my mom with Grandpa there beside her—playing croquet, walking on the beach, burying each other in the sand next to the ocean, and looking out at the Statue of Liberty from the top of the Empire State Building. Grandpa seemed to be an intimate part of my mom and dad's young family—all while Grandma walked alone at the back of the family and Dad kept the camera rolling.

On one road trip to Mexico, Dad's silent film captured Grandpa flirting with Mom, walking side by side through the native temple ruins in their own little world, Grandma once again trailing many feet behind. Grandpa walked next to Mom and captivated her with his casual charm. The energy was palpable. To an outside observer, this could have been Mom and Grandpa's honeymoon. Dad kept filming while Mom stood next to Grandpa on a romantic boat ride down the coast of Mexico, looking out across the ocean as her hair blew in the warm breeze.

Dad mentioned this Mexico trip in his own memoir. He described lying in his hotel room too weak to move, confined there by Montezuma's revenge. At one point, he summoned his energy and pulled himself to the hotel window to look out at the beach. To his dismay, he discovered his own dad walking hand-in-hand with his bride along the beautiful Mexican shoreline, leaving footprints that would be washed away with the coming tide but couldn't be washed away from Dad's heart—or Mom's conscience.

Dad knew Mom and Grandpa had a special friendship—he also knew Grandpa was a "cad," as Grandma said—a magnet for the ladies. But seeing his own dad with his wife on the beach in Mexico enraged him.

On the way home, after safely crossing the Mexican-American border, Dad angrily stopped the car on the side of the road and let Grandpa have it.

"How could you do this to your own son?" he yelled.

"Oh, it's nothing," my mom said apologetically as Dad seethed. I'm sure it was an ugly scene, but Mom continued, "Don't worry about it."

Although Dad never said another word to Mom about the Mexican beach, I'm sure he continued to feel troubled by his dad's relationship with her. But instead of confronting Mom again, he kept taking silent home movies of the love of his life.

And Grandpa hung out at our house when Dad wasn't home—which was often, since Dad was so busy with his work and church responsibilities. Mom and Grandpa would talk for hours and hours like best friends, confiding their deepest secrets in each other. Mom would challenge Grandpa in Indian leg wrestling, and Grandpa would help her get the kids off to bed.

I remember Grandpa sometimes lying next to Mom on her bed—Mom and Dad's bed, that is—or sitting close to her on our couch or staying up late with her on camping trips. They seemed to be joined at the hip whenever Grandpa was around.

Grandpa provided companionship for my mom when Dad was away—or did he just lure her with his charm until my mom couldn't say *no*? Rumor has it that many women were lured in by Grandpa's charm.

Although I rationalized when I got older that Mom was close to Grandpa because her own dad died when she was just twenty-five, the sordid relationship had started many years before that—when Mom was just twelve and Grandpa was a dad and a youth leader who should have known better. The chemistry between Grandpa and Mom was plain to see in Dad's silent home movies—but we all took a vow of silence to never speak about it.

25

Let There Be Light

Jane broke that vow of silence. Shortly after she married Dad, Jane announced to me that Grandpa had indeed seduced Mom. She shared the rumors that had been shared with her.

What was I supposed to do with them? What was I supposed to think? How was I supposed to feel? Was Mom really an adulteress? I learned in church and seminary and the scriptures that adultery was second only to murder—and now Jane was telling me my mom had done *both*? I had heard this rumor before, but I hadn't believed it, and now I tried to push the thought aside.

But the whispering continued. And when Grandpa impregnated his third-oldest son's wife and divorced Grandma to marry his daughter-in-law eighteen months after my mom died, the rumors seemed more plausible. I still loved Grandpa, but I was confused by this horrible thought. And I was even more confused by Dad's silent acceptance. Dad even hired Grandpa as the accountant for his business.

In one reflective moment, Grandpa told me about Mom and how wonderful she was. He clearly missed her. He told me that he knew what the rumors were, but he said that he wouldn't talk about his relationship with Mom because she wasn't around to defend herself. His light-blue eyes gazed into the distance, and he said, "No one can judge the heart."

It seemed to me that this was a confession, but I remained silent too.

According to Dad's memoir, shortly after Mom's death, Mom's

oldest sister told my father, "It was your dad! Linda came out the night before she died and said she couldn't handle it anymore."

The rumors continued. Someone told me that they suspected Mom took her life because she couldn't face the public humiliation of church discipline for infidelity while Dad served in a leadership position. But after talking with Grandpa's second wife years later, Dad became certain that Mom's relationship with Grandpa was strictly emotional.

Whatever the extent of Mom's relationship with Grandpa, my heart tells me that she died not because she was afraid to face church discipline but because her world was dark. She couldn't feel Jesus Christ's redeeming love—the love that redeems not only from sin but from pain, sickness, heartache, and death. She had experienced the peace and light of the next life when she'd visited there six months earlier, and she must have longed for that reunion of love. She must have felt that our family would be better off without her, or she wouldn't have pulled the trigger. She couldn't have pulled the trigger feeling otherwise.

Dad certainly felt rejected when he saw Mom walk hand in hand with Grandpa on the Mexican seashore. How did he feel about Mom's request for Grandpa to meet them when her heart failed or Grandpa's offer for Mom to stay with him after her cardiac arrest? Dad must have been deeply hurt.

Surely, the ultimate rejection came when Dad saw Mom lying face-up in a pool of blood in the bathroom with his rifle next to her lifeless body.

As I contemplate my memories and the memories others have shared of my mom—a woman of strength, life, sunshine, laughter, service, and faith, a best friend to all who knew her—I wonder how Mom could have been led away by her own father-in-law. How could she walk hand-in-hand with him on the beach in Mexico? And how was it that a man who shared so much brightness with little children could stoop to rob the wives from his two sons?

How could a grandma tie her grandchildren, whom she loved, to kitchen chairs? How could a babysitter sexually abuse a young girl? How could a dad threaten his own son with a belt? How could a precocious ten-year-old boy turn to alcohol? How could a husband beat his wife with a two-by-four? How could a mom pull the trigger?

How can there be so much darkness in broad daylight?

We read in Genesis:

In the beginning God created the heaven and the earth. And the earth was without form, and void; and darkness was upon the face of the deep. . . . And God said, Let there be light: and there was light. And God saw the light, that it was good: and God divided the light from the darkness. (Genesis 1:3–4)

God didn't take away the darkness, but he provided a light—and he separated it from the darkness.

Within each of us, we find both darkness and light, and we work our whole lives to do what God did in the very beginning—to divide the light from the darkness. To unbury our hearts, to remove the dark dirt and the rocks that bind us so that our wounds can be cleansed by the giver of light, Jesus Christ.

It is Jesus Christ to whom we can give our darkest night. We can give him the darkness of adultery or suicide or sexual abuse or anger, and his love can heal our hearts. He can carry our deepest pains, our greatest sorrows, and our heaviest burdens. He can lift us from the darkest abyss and carry us to the light. Then we can feel His love. Then we can see our own brightness. Then we can love.

26

Coming Home

MARCH 2011

"John, I feel like I'm going crazy," I blurted out. "I can't stop crying. I can't think straight. I can't focus on work, and I need to be able to focus!"

I had ripped off the yucky, stinky bandage from my heart and removed a few rocks to take a peek inside, and now dirt was spilling out. I couldn't contain the tears.

"John, I want to pile the rocks back on. I want to close the lid on all the pain. But I can't. And my heart hurts."

My heart, which I had carefully protected all these years with piles of rocks and dirt, was now gripped with stabbing pain, raw and bleeding, where my mom had shot me.

"I can't get it together. I can't turn my brain off or stop thinking about my mom, and I feel like I'm going to explode!" I cried.

That morning, before my appointment with John, I'd stood in my office, unable to move, staring blankly out the door when one of my nurses, Leili, passed by.

"Wendy, are you okay?" she asked, concern in her voice.

"Do you have a minute to talk?" I answered, panic and fear in my heart as I thought of the details of Mom's death—the blood, picking up Annie from her crib, finding out she shot herself, the nightmares, everything. And I couldn't make it stop. My brain was all jumbled—but I had so much to do! Sixty-five nurses depended on me to lead them, and I was in no condition to work.

129

"Of course," she answered.

"Leili, I can't do my work," I sobbed in her arms. "My brain is a mess. I'm a mess," I shared the journey I had begun with John.

I had skillfully hidden my heart from the nurses who worked for me. I protected intimate details of my past with a carefully placed mask. A few days earlier I had risked sharing with Blake and Melissa, and now I shared a fragmented story with Leili.

"My mom shot herself. I was twelve. I'm in therapy. I can't think. My therapist thinks I have PTSD," I said, half-crazed. "I don't want a diagnosis!"

A mental health diagnosis was the last thing I wanted. My mom must have had mental health problems—and she shot herself. *I don't want a diagnosis!* I thought again.

"Do *you* think you have PTSD?" Leili asked.

"I don't know. I can't sleep. I can't concentrate. I have nightmares. I'm terrified of dying." *I'm afraid of the dark and germs and medicine and strangers and heights and needles and hospitals and knives and guns and—and ghosts.*

"I don't know. Maybe." I choked back the tears.

"How can you do everything that you do if you have PTSD?" Leili countered. "You're a successful manager. You take care of your home and your husband and your family and us. You do so much. How can you do it all if you have PTSD?" She paused, shook her head, and answered her own question. "No," she said.

"If you look at all the symptoms and the diagnostic criteria," I argued, putting my nurse hat on to look at myself, "then yes, it looks like I could have PTSD. But I don't want a diagnosis!"

"Wendy, don't let your therapist put thoughts in your mind," Leili cautioned. "You'll be okay."

She hugged me again and left me to think of her warning. And yet, I felt disconnected from myself—like I was on the outside looking in. And what I saw was craziness. I couldn't stop thinking about Mom or blood or ghosts. I had shared the secret I once protected, and now I wanted to scream.

John, help me fix myself! I screamed in my head as I stared at him. I felt like I did when I walked home late at night by myself as a young girl—my eyes darting in the blackness, trying to see the monster lurking behind a tree, ready to jump out and snatch me away. My eyes wouldn't focus in the dark, but I could sense the danger, and I started at the slightest rustle of leaves overhead. Now, sitting in John's office, I expressed the terror I felt.

"John, I feel like I'm twelve years old again," I said, knowing full well that a part of me was frozen in time—a part of me never did grow up. And now, as I tried to reconcile the past with the present, I couldn't bring my two selves together into one whole.

"Wendy, I've had other patients tell me that they've felt how you feel. But as awful as you feel right now, you are exactly where you need to be," John explained. "You're thinking about your mom and talking about your mom and uncovering the wound that you buried all those years ago. You're cleaning out the infection. So even though it hurts right now, this is an important part of healing. It's called exposure therapy. Talking desensitizes you to the trauma of your mom's death. If you'd had the chance to talk about your mom's death when you were twelve, you wouldn't have these lasting wounds. But you were the good soldier. You bandaged up the wound as best you could and kept on marching."

I left John's office with the assignment to keep scrubbing.

Some might compare losing one's mind to turning off a light switch—going from light to utter darkness. To me, it felt like every switch in my brain was turned on at once. It felt like a blinding brightness. Everywhere I turned—everything I saw—reminded me of Mom. As I tried to run from the ghosts, I lost more pebbles with every step, and a trail of blood marked my path.

Even if I wanted to, I couldn't turn off the blinding lights.

※ ※

On Thursday, March 3, 2011, I wrote in my journal: "Uncle Bob's funeral. I felt grown-up. Like I had come home."

Thirty-six years earlier, tall, slender, vitamin-and-herb-consuming vegetarian Uncle Bob had come home to care for his baby sister, Linda, who had just returned from the sweet escape of death. Dad had begged Bob, who lived in Arizona, to come to Mom's bedside at Grandpa's home, where she remained caught between Earth and heaven following her cardiac arrest. Although Mom wouldn't go to a doctor or the hospital, she trusted Bob's experience with natural healing. Bob arrived with teas, tinctures, a canister of oxygen, and a prescription for sunshine aimed at restoring Mom's vitality.

Bob had advised Mom on her health since she was fifteen, when she visited him in Wyoming a few years after he graduated from a chiropractic-naturopathic school. Mom wrote to Dad from Bob's Wyoming home on April 10, 1959:

> Bob worked on me for an hour or so. Gosh, I didn't realize how much he could tell about me just by feeling my stomach. This is about all I got from what he said was wrong with me: one of my main arteries to my heart is half shut, not letting the blood circulate through my body sufficiently, thus making me have sharp pains in the left side of my chest.
>
> He showed me what I could do to help it. Then he worked on my back and said that the 5th something was really out, and he popped it and it really made a loud noise. It sure feels a hundred percent better than it did. Here in this building, the part Bob lives in, there are about twelve bathtubs. This is 'cause people, or Bob's patients, take a steam bath, then a mineral bath. Boy, the water smells just like the pipe plant, but I am getting used to it. Everyone was taking a steam bath and a mineral bath but me, and I don't think I will. However, I might, as Bob wants me to. He said I am nervous and it would really help to calm my nerves. Bob looked in my eyes and told me that I was nervous and had had some lung trouble at one time, and lots of things. Oh Darling, you have been wanting me to have a check-up. Well, Bob gave me a thorough one. Oh, I can't eat so much bread, so you can help me remember, okay?

She closed with:

> P.S. I love you, darling. XOXOX for when I get home. Take care of yourself, and eat good meals each day, won't you?

Two years after Mom visited Uncle Bob in Wyoming, Mom's own mom died in a Utah hospital under the care of nurses and doctors, cementing Mom's lifelong fear of traditional medicine. Mom turned instead to the medicine of her oldest brother, who had correctly diagnosed her heart condition, which later proved nearly fatal.

Now, thirty-six years later, we were going to Bob's graveside service.

"Let me just grab my shoes," I said to Dad, who had come to pick me up. As usual, I was running a few minutes behind. I had to put on the last touches of makeup, comb my dripping-wet hair, grab my shoes and coat, and run to the car parked in the driveway where Jane was waiting.

"Sorry to be late," I said as I hopped in the backseat of the car. I was nervous about Jane's disapproval. She hated it when people were late, and it seemed like I was always late. But I was a grown-up now, and Jane was an older lady, softened somewhat by life and medication. I still felt vulnerable, though, and I protected myself with an emotional distance.

I looked out the window. Double-yellow lines divided a busy street crowded with houses, schools, grocery stores, and streetlights, but I saw the same trees and white lines of thirty-six years ago—this time without procession. No lights. No limousine. No hearse. We entered the cemetery that overlooked the valley on a paved road instead of a dirt one. We parked and walked toward the small group gathered on the hillside next to a little white building. There were no flowers or green straps, and there was no casket. Dad reminded me that Mom's parents were buried on the next row over. "Yep," I muttered in response. No mention of Mom. I barely glanced down the hill toward her headstone a block away.

It was overcast on this March afternoon, and the ground was still brown and moist from the long, cold winter. The trees were bare but would soon bud a glorious green to welcome the birds' return. Already, a few chirps tested the miracle of rebirth. The evergreen trees were now so big that they blocked the view of the lake from Grandma Eva's headstone. Few cars had traveled the road below thirty-six years ago. Now the distant roar of cars hurrying people back from their lunch breaks replaced the quiet and solitude of the cemetery I'd visited on my bike when I was twelve.

Bob had been cremated in Arizona, and his children weren't quite sure what to do for a memorial. He had been absent from their life for decades. His wife divorced him before the youngest of their three children was in grade school. Although Bob was a gifted healer, he was not a gifted businessman, and he couldn't adequately provide for his family. He'd moved to Arizona chasing one multi-level scheme after another, hoping to strike gold. He continued to take his vitamins and herbs and drink his teas and other concoctions, which Jane attributed to his longevity compared to his five younger brothers and sisters who died before they reached sixty-five. Only three of the nine siblings remained alive.

Thanks to the urging of my cousin, Jackie, Bob's burnt remains were transported back to Utah and had been laid to rest in a tiny plot of ground under two twisted trees in Mom's cemetery. We gathered to witness the dedication of that dirt, and we resurrected the beautiful memories of a family that used to gather for lively family activities in the sunshine each month—winter, spring, summer, and fall—but now only gathered for deaths. *Who would be next?* we all wondered. We promised to plan a family reunion before the next funeral—a commitment of reconnection, a rekindling of love and light and laughter. Another resurrection.

With great effort, Mom's last living sister, gray-haired Grace, made her way across the bumpy, still-dead grass, clutching her husband's arm to steady herself. Someone told me that Grace had pancreatic cysts that weren't cancer but were worrisome nonetheless. She suffered from severe back pain yet faithfully attended each funeral and wedding.

My cousin Karen, who used to babysit me, hung to Suzette, her younger sister and nurse. She walked slowly, catching her breath every few steps. Her lips were tinged bluish-gray. She'd needed oxygen since her stroke, but she didn't want to wear it in public.

Cousin Cindy came with a video camera to record the service for her dad, who was too ill to travel the forty-five minutes to the cemetery. Don was confined to his home, recovering from brain surgery, and his wife suffered from dementia. Cindy limped into place next to Karen. Despite severe pain and an extended hospitalization after being hit by a drunk driver months before, Cindy took care of her mom and dad. She struggled to stand for the short service, but she recorded every detail she could so that Don could grieve for his brother's death in the privacy of his own home.

Marie walked up the hill toward us, and Annie came from the opposite direction with her nine-year-old daughter. We were outsiders who wanted desperately to belong. Dad had accompanied Mom to her frequent and celebrated family gatherings from the time he was fifteen. Every child at those events had felt welcomed and loved by Grandma Eva, whom I never knew, and sang "Horsey-Horsey On Your Way" with Grandpa Rowley, who died when I was six. Dad came to reunite with this family who had once taken him in as one of their own, and Jane stood by his side, wrapped in her sweaters and scarves and coat, encouraging his reconnection.

We soaked up the love of this family we no longer knew. We'd stopped attending the family activities shortly after Mom died, but the warm memories remained in my heart. And I longed to belong again. This family welcomed me home with open arms as I talked with cousin after cousin and sensed the longing in their hearts too—longing for reunion with lost loved ones living and dead. Though each person carried their own wounds—wounds of past hurts and present illnesses—there was an immediate connection, a bond that does not break even in death. And I did belong.

Three soldiers stood at attention among the trees, ready to give a final salute to Uncle Bob, who served faithfully in the Marines during World War II in the Pacific Islands. Rick, Bob's youngest son, shared a few words about his dad, and someone offered a prayer. The words were quickly forgotten, but healing love wove through the trees like a big ribbon of golden-white light that tied the entire family together. It touched our hearts and seeped into our souls, planting seeds next to our scars that, if nourished, would transform our hurts and heal our hearts. We hesitated to leave.

27

The Lady I Could Never Call Mom

It's hard for one household to have two moms. Whom do you listen to? Whom do you obey? Who has ultimate decision-making authority?

Of course, I felt like I did. After all, I was Mom's right arm. So when Mom died, it was only natural that I should assume my rightful place next to Dad at the head of the family. And Dad expected that I would do all sorts of motherly things—babysit until late at night, change diapers, get the kids in their pajamas, and chase them to bed. I'm certain he didn't expect, though, that before bedtime I would make out on the red shag family-room carpet with the neighbor boy up the street while my little brothers and sisters fought over the TV next to me or ran around the room.

I had an open-door policy. When Dad was out with Jane escaping the chaos, all friends and neighbors were invited over for the fun and freedom of a parentless home. Jane's daughter, Sally, raised until now as a single daughter, hid from all the commotion in her bedroom in my haunted basement.

Sally's bedroom was in the room once dedicated to play, complete with a keyed lock on her door—to protect her from us, I guess. No one

137

was allowed in her bedroom except Jane, who spent hours with Sally while she created clay sculptures and artistic drawings suitable for framing. And no one was allowed in the master bedroom—no one, that is, except Sally. A new lock kept out all other intruders and protected Dad's new girls. But who would protect the rest of us from a wicked stepmom? Who would protect us from pain and fear and rejection and abandonment and anger and hate? Who would protect me from ghostly hauntings?

Dad worked all the time—and when he wasn't working, he was "working on his relationship" with Jane and Sally. Dad dragged all of us to counseling—not to process Mom's suicide, but to learn how to obey Jane and understand the "consequences" of disobedience. Sadly, consequences escalated to punishment and even abuse, especially for my sisters.

"Dad!" I argued passionately one day as I sat next to him in the front seat of our van, "She's a terrible mom! Why don't you just get a divorce?"

Dad stared straight ahead as he drove me to a school function. I pleaded for Dad to understand the abuse that Jane inflicted when he wasn't home.

"She hit Marie! She made her bleed!" I cried.

"Marie must have done something to deserve it," Dad said flatly as he continued straight ahead.

"Nobody deserves that, Dad!" I stared at him while he drove, hoping for any sort of understanding.

"She puts Annie in time-out for hours! She yanks Marie out of school if her bed isn't made! She yells at us! She's mean and awful!"

"You kids need to mind better," Dad countered, still driving.

"She's *crazy!*"

"She's under a lot of stress. We just need to be patient with her."

Be patient with her? What about us?!

"She *hates* us!" I yelled.

Nothing.

"Dad, she doesn't love you either!"

Silence.

"Why don't you leave her?"

But instead of leaving Jane, Dad left us. He clung to Jane and Sally, afraid to lose a second wife and his new daughter. He begged aunts and uncles and neighbors and friends to watch after us so Jane could have a break. He shipped Marie from home to home trying to make Jane happy.

Through the years, every single child of Dad's was asked to leave. I was asked to go live with Aunt Bea in California for a summer when I was eighteen, after Dad realized he couldn't send me away on a semester abroad. While I was gone, Jane moved my things to an apartment I had never seen before. Cary spent days and weeks and sometimes months with friends after mom's death and was permanently kicked out at eighteen. After being shuffled from place to place from the time she was eight, Marie was on her own at sixteen. Drew was kicked out after Jane came home and found him watching a movie with a bunch of his friends—boys and girls with their arms around each other. He was just seventeen and still in high school when he was moved to an apartment. And at fifteen years old, Dad banished Annie to the cabin down the hill from the house he'd bought for Jane. Annie lived alone in that cabin. She described walking up the long hill to the parents' home and knocking on the door to "beg for food like a dog." Jane made Annie stand on the porch and wait for her to hand food through a narrow crack in the screen door.

Dad argued that we weren't obedient and that Jane couldn't handle us. He was right. After losing our mom to suicide and our dad to Jane, we each just tried to survive. We made bad choices. We got in trouble. But still, he could have tried to protect us—at least from the pain, fear, rejection, abandonment, anger, and hate. He could have allowed us in his bedroom in the middle of the night to protect us from ghostly hauntings, instead of making us knock on a locked door that opened just a crack. He could have protected us from a wicked stepmother.

Instead, protection was left up to me. So I stuffed down my fear and tried to protect my brothers and sisters from Jane.

Jane was scholarly and strict. She had bachelor's and master's degrees in fine arts. She worked as an illustrator, and her parents, Grampy and Grammy, took care of Sally while Jane worked. They loved, doted on, and spoiled her. Sally could do no wrong by the time she entered our home. Jane made sure to "train" Sally. She bragged about shoving Sally's head under cold running water in the bathtub if she disobeyed. "Just like the Indians did," Jane told me.

She set about to "train" us too—us wild, unrefined, ferocious hellions. When Jane wasn't hiding under the bed or in a closet, yelling at us from the top of the stairs, or cowering in a corner during one of her manic-depressive episodes, she incessantly criticized and rebuked. When her episodes got really bad, she thought we might take up arms against her in open rebellion.

"We *were*, not we *was*!" Jane snapped, correcting the grammar we had learned from our stay-at-home mom, who had taught us how to can peaches, pit cherries, bake bread, and plant gardens instead of grading our homework. Not that Mom wasn't committed to scholastic excellence—she was. She helped me with my math and spelling homework and expected me to do my very best. She was proud that I was in the advanced reading class in elementary school and won the school spelling bee in fifth grade. Mom volunteered in the PTA and brought treats to our class. She'd hauled a preschooler and a baby to school to bring in live lobsters in a wash basin for a class show-and-tell.

After the pictures of Mom were removed, Jane set out to undo all the damage our dead mom had inflicted upon us. But she was trying to maintain control of a classroom where she didn't want to teach. Jane told us we were rude, didn't know how to eat, and didn't have any manners. "Keep your elbows off the table! Chew with your mouth closed! Say 'please'! Say 'thank you'!" It didn't matter that Mom taught me how to set a table perfectly, to Indian leg wrestle, to drive a stick shift, dig in the dirt, hold a baby, ride a motorcycle, camp, and say my prayers every single night. It didn't matter that Mom had loved me. Even when I didn't say *please* or *thank you*, she loved me and I loved her. I missed her. But this lady who I could never call *Mom* hated me. She didn't want me to be her right arm. I could never win her affection, adoration, or acceptance—and especially not her love.

Mostly Jane ignored me. She was afraid of me. I stood up for my siblings as their protector. I yelled back at Jane when I thought she'd crossed the line with her discipline. I inserted myself when I thought she'd misbehaved. I even tried to teach her how to load a dishwasher. But she hid in her locked bedroom. She protected herself with a dark energy that encircled her and kept any light she might share from escaping. Although I was terrified of her and her constant belittling, I was determined to shelter my brothers and sisters from her darkness. Every ounce of anger I had stored up in my heart was directed at Jane—the lady I could never call *Mom*. And she maintained a safe distance—continents apart despite standing in the same room.

Who was she to take my baby sister from me, to cut off her curls and give her a bath only once a week? Who was she to neglect Annie's basic hygiene, to refuse to potty train her and then spank her after learning that Annie went to the bathroom outside at preschool? Who was she to slap me across the face and scratch me with her nails after she yelled at me about the boys my best friend and I were talking to in our backyard? But I could fight back. I could yell and scream as loud as she could. I could protect myself from her blows, so she never struck me again.

But I remained fearful of Jane—terrified that she would ridicule and criticize. When I was expecting my first baby shortly after marrying my husband at age nineteen, Jane disapproved of my pregnancy. And she fought her way into my dreams, attacking me with a knife to cut out and kill my unborn baby.

I hated her. At the very least, I was afraid of her. Jane adopted Marie, Drew, and Annie when she married Dad, but she refused to adopt me and Cary. And while Dad adopted Sally and loved her like he never did his own children, Jane considered Cary and me to be too grown-up and set in our ways, and she didn't want any responsibility for us. Or maybe she was just afraid too.

Two years after they were married, Jane was traveling to Hawaii with Dad on a business trip, and she wrote me a letter. It was her first attempt to connect with an independent almost-fifteen-year-old who had a hole in her heart covered with rocks and dirt. She wrote:

> Dear Wendy,
>
> This might surprise you to get a letter from me. I have been wanting to write this letter for a long time, but just never have. And I thought to myself, "This time I will." So I am writing it. It will not be easy. I think especially it will not be easy for you to know how to take it, maybe, or to react to it. But I have noticed lately that you really have been "growing up" a lot and that is great, and so I take this chance.
>
> I don't know if I ever will say very much, but I am better at writing—and I just wanted you to know that I did appreciate you and I see you growing up into really a nice person, and I admire you for a lot of things.
>
> You and I never did have a very good chance to have good feelings about each other, and I think it's perfectly understandable, and I'm willing to accept it—because of the position we've been put in. The "wicked stepmother" thing wasn't just made up out of the blue. It was a normal thing and probably always will be. Even real "mothers and daughters" have a hard time during the teenage years. And for "unreal" mothers and

daughters, it's doubly hard. And I finally gave up (as you could see and still can) trying to be a mother to you. It was sad you lost your mother. Really sad, and I just feel heartbroken about that. But no one can ever be expected to take her place.

Maybe for a grown-up person, to be afraid is a silly thing. But I am afraid (I know your dad has told you this). I am not afraid of grown-up people because I trust them more. As you grow up more, I think I will be able to trust you more, and maybe I will not be so afraid. I feel bad I cannot step in as an adult "mother" and help you where you may need it (although I feel you are doing really well without one, truly), but I can't.

Although it is still risky and frightening, I guess I always will keep trying—and I am sort of really trying right now in a way, Wendy, because I just wanted to let you know that I do care.

I really do care. I ache all the times I am not able to give you any support or encouragement because of my own fears. I would like to be able to give more praise and to help—maybe even to share—but it is really hard, and maybe it will never happen—but at least I can keep trying in safe ways (like writing notes or letters?) or just being quiet and trying to care from a distance.

Please forgive me for my silence, Wendy. I pray you might understand. I even may not change—but I wanted you to know I do care. I do care. I do think you are a lovely girl. And I want you to be happy.

Please don't expect a lot. I think you've been doing just fine, and I admire how you have gone on without a mother—a hard thing to do.

You have a lot going for you, Wendy. You really do. Keep up the good work.

Always, your (distant) friend
(but wanting to be your friend)
Jane

I was confused by this letter from the lady I could never call *Mom.* I did go on without a mother. I kept my distance just as she kept hers. Over the years, Jane did reach out again from time to time with a note or a letter. She was the historian for our family. She compiled a yearly calendar with pictures of happy times and encouraged Dad to preserve memories of Mom—love letters, genealogy, home movies, and pictures. She even edited Dad's memoir. Eventually, when I was a grandma, Jane offered a warm embrace and lovingly held my grandchildren on her lap, but she couldn't mother while we were still children.

Maybe no one could mother five motherless children.

28

BIG—and little

"Dinner!" Dad hollered down the stairs. I jumped up from the chair in the family room and ran toward the stairs leading up to the kitchen. In my hurry, I misjudged the space between the stairs and didn't leave enough room for my left hand. As I leapt on the first stair, my hand smacked the wall at the bottom of the stairs, sending stabs of pain through my hand and up my arm. I instinctively grabbed my hand and doubled over in pain, crying out for my dad. I collapsed on the stairs, unable to walk.

"Dad! Dad!" I yelled, trying to push back the tears. "I think I broke my hand."

"Here, let me look at it," Dad said matter-of-factly.

Trying to brace my injured hand against my body, I held it close to my stomach with my right hand. I breathed heavily as Dad inspected my hand.

"I think it's okay," he declared. "Let's just see how it does over the next few days."

"But Dad," I argued, "I've had broken bones before. I know how it feels. I think my hand is broken."

"No, I think it's okay," Dad insisted. "Let's just watch it."

Dad was busy trying to hold his marriage together. He worked long hours, and when he got home from work, he scolded children for not obeying Jane. The last thing he wanted to deal with was a broken hand.

Almost eight years earlier, Mom had rushed me to the hospital when I screamed out in pain after Aunt Cheri dropped my four-year

143

old brother on my arm. I was almost six, and I was lying on the concrete steps that led to Grandma and Grandpa's house in Illinois. Aunt Cheri teased me while she dangled Cary above my head.

"You better move, or I'm going to drop him," Cheri said as she swung Cary high in the air, holding onto an arm and a leg.

I laughed and laughed—and didn't move. Suddenly, after a big swing, Cheri let go, and Cary came crashing down on my left arm. I screamed out in pain, and my mom ran from inside the house to my side. I cried and cried while Mom and Grandpa rushed me to the hospital emergency room. She tried to quiet me by pointing out another girl waiting in the emergency room with a badly misshapen arm. That little girl had fallen from a bicycle and her arm looked worse than mine, so I didn't need to cry anymore.

After x-rays, the doctor showed us where I broke my arm in three places. He wrapped cool, wet strips of cast material from my fingertips to my armpit and gave me a sling to protect the hardening cast. It wasn't long before I was running and playing with my brother again, my casted arm covered in plastic to play in the sprinklers.

The year before Mom died, I'd slid into first base and landed on my hand with my fingers bent under my wrist. I was in excruciating pain, so Mom again took me to the hospital. Sure enough, my ulna and radius were broken at my left wrist.

Now, a year later, Mom was gone and Dad wanted to "wait and see." I knew my hand was broken. It felt broken, and it began to swell. Several days after my exciting run up the stairs, my hand was twice its normal size and black and blue. I couldn't move my fingers, and I had a constant throbbing pain even though I tried to hold my hand up to decrease the swelling. Dad finally consented to take me to the hospital emergency room.

The doctor took x-rays and showed us where the third knuckle of my left pinkie finger was broken off and pushed over to the knuckle at the bottom of my ring finger. Since we had waited, the bone was already trying to knit back together—only it wasn't where it should be. The doctor took my hand and pushed as hard as he could on my broken knuckle to see if he could set it by pushing it back where it belonged. The pain was nearly unbearable and my vision blurred, but by now I knew I shouldn't cry. The doctor put a cast on my arm and told us to come back in a week for another x-ray to see if my knuckle would miraculously heal.

"Dad, I *knew* it was broken," I said in an "I told you so" sort of way on the way out of the emergency room.

The next week, Dad and I returned to the emergency room doctor, who took another set of x-rays. No miracle. My black-and-blue hand was still swollen, it still hurt, and I needed surgery to move the bone fragment back in place and pins to keep it there. Now instead of one trip to the ER when I first hurt my hand, I headed to the hospital for the third time—this time to be put to sleep.

Dad checked me in and said good-bye, and a nurse took me to a room with a hospital bed and instructed me to take off all my clothes and put on a hospital gown.

"Even my underwear?" I asked.

"Everything needs to be sterile in the operating room," the nurse explained matter-of-factly, "so take everything off."

Why does everything need to come off if they're just operating on my hand? I wondered to myself as I slowly changed out of my clothes. *Who will keep me covered when they put me to sleep?* The floor was cold. The bed was cold. I couldn't even get warm with the blanket wrapped tightly around my legs.

I was scared to be put to sleep, and I didn't want to let go of the blanket, but I was obedient when the nurse told me to move from the bed to the operating table. I kept my legs tightly closed while the nurse started an IV, and then I was out.

Nothingness.

✖ ✖

"We can't get a pulse on her!" someone said frantically.

"Is she breathing?" another person asked.

"Someone help me; we can't get a pulse!"

Everything was black and heavy. I couldn't move. I couldn't talk. I couldn't open my eyes. I was paralyzed.

I'm alive! I wanted to scream. But I couldn't move.

People swarmed to my bed to try to rouse me. I hovered in darkness to the left of where the commotion was—my bed to the right seemed very far away. Someone shook me. I felt nothing. I saw nothing.

I'm alive! I screamed in my head. But no one heard.

I slipped to sleep and woke briefly to a nurse's hands on my face, lifting my jaw to help me breathe.

"It's time to wake up, Wendy," said the nurse, gently shaking me. "The surgery is over. It's time to wake up now." With great effort, I opened my eyes for a moment but could not will my eyelids to stay up. Too tired to move. Too heavy. Too dark.

Slowly, I became aware of my hand suspended in the air above me—tied to a metal bar above my head. My eyes flickered open, then closed again. Time to sleep some more.

I awoke next in my hospital room, my hand still hanging above me, wrapped in layers of bandages. It didn't resemble a hand or feel like one—it was still numb and dead from the surgery. It looked more like a big, white club detached from my body.

Like my hand, my heart remained tightly bandaged. I had tried to numb the pain with friends and music and late nights and boys and motorcycles, but now I lay confined to a bed in a gray hospital room—alone.

The nurse plopped a steak dinner in front of me and immediately left the room. I stared at the hunk of meat from where I lay with my head propped up and wondered how I was supposed to eat it with one of my hands still suspended in the air. Should I just pick up the whole thing with one working hand and start gnawing on it?

Dad and Jane came to visit for a short time. Then I was left to myself again—alone but alive.

Mom had always cared for me when I was sick or hurt or afraid. She held my hair back when I threw up in the toilet. She put cool compresses on my forehead when I was burning up with a fever. She prepared a warm baking soda bath for me when I broke out with the chicken pox and told me not to pick at the scabs when they started to itch. She made a cayenne pepper concoction for me to gargle when I had tonsillitis, and she put an onion poultice around my neck that made my eyes water when I had the flu.

Now, after my first hospital stay—where they couldn't find a pulse through my bandaged heart, where I was alive and dead at the same time—I was released to my own care. Dad picked me up and took me home, but I was responsible to do my own dressing changes and to clean the pin site exactly as instructed several times a day.

Mom was gone.

As much as I wanted Mom to put a cool compress on my forehead, Mom would never touch my forehead again. I was a grown-up now and could bandage my own hurts. I had lots of practice. With all the experience of my thirteen years, I was perfectly capable of caring for myself. I could take care of a house full of little kids, I could clean out my mom's clothes, I could pick out headstones, and I could bandage my heart. Of course I could look after my own hand.

And I could travel the world by myself just a few months later—walking down the streets of New York City with three girlfriends at seven in the morning, smiling innocently at the older men who were already removing trash and climbing in sewer holes and opening newspaper stands. From New York to London to Amsterdam to Belgium to Paris to Geneva, hiking in the Alps and walking through the Louvre, stealing a kiss from my first true love behind piles of skeletons in the catacombs. I was grown up. "Let them eat cake" echoed in my ears in Marie Antoinette's village, her chateau sitting majestically at the water's edge. Freedom!

My mask firmly in place, I could do anything. I was invincible. I could fly down the slopes on my red-white-and-blue K-2 Comp skis in the winter and glide on the water on my slalom ski behind the boat I called mine in the summer. I could ride through the air on a motorcycle and hike to the tallest peak in the still-dark foothills behind our home to see the sunrise. Of course I could take care of my hand.

Never mind that I didn't know how to curl my hair, put on makeup, change a tampon, or zap my zits. I had friends who did. I learned to slather on dark base so I could have an eternal suntan (though I wish someone would have taught me about blending in the line at the bottom of my chin) and apply white eye cream up to my eyebrow and down to my cheekbone—kind of like a reverse raccoon—then smear the greasy blue stick on my eyelids. I never did learn how to keep mascara from smudging, though. The red blush accented my best feature—the cheeks I got from my mom. And shiny lip gloss highlighted my wide smile.

When I cut my toe on a glass bottle in the bathroom of the Paris hotel our school group was staying at, I didn't cry. I simply limped with Bill, my first true love, to my French professor's room and asked for a bandage. When the creepy professor asked Bill to leave so the teacher could care for me alone, I pleaded with my eyes for Bill to stay. *Don't leave me alone with this pervert!* I cried in my head. He couldn't keep his hands off the female students. He was always rubbing their backs and looking down their shirts, and I wasn't about to stay there alone in his hotel room.

"I just need a bandage," I said out loud. "I can take care of it."

I was big. And grown-up.

And little.

I felt little at Christmastime when I put Mom's Angie the angel on top of the little tree in my bedroom. I sat on the floor, listening to my Christmas records while the tree lights' colors melted together like multi-colored hot fudge topping through my tear-filled eyes.

I felt little every time a boy broke my tightly wrapped heart. I cried in my bedroom, played my guitar, and felt sick to my stomach. I couldn't eat, couldn't sleep, and couldn't get out of bed—I couldn't move. I wanted to die too.

I felt little when I was in my first year of college and saw a show about a sister who dies. After the show on December 8, 1980, I wrote:

> It was so sad, and shows like that always make me think about my mom, and I sometimes wish so bad that she was still here and that I could put my arms around her and tell her how much I love her and that I could share my college experiences and my love life with her and confide in her and not be afraid of what I told her because I knew she would always love me no matter what.

One time when I was sixteen, I uncovered my heart just enough to share with my high school sweetheart how my mom died. My religion teacher taught that suicide was murder and that there would be no for-giveness—Mom would go to hell. I told my boyfriend the story with no emotion and quickly replaced the bandages so the rocks wouldn't fall out. He assured me that Mom would not go to hell. But I didn't know where she was—I just knew she couldn't bandage my hurts any more. Bandaging was left to me.

I felt little and big and *crazy* when at sixteen I tried to end my life by driving my little red Honda as fast as I could in the church parking lot and crashing into the curb. I had visions of my car flipping in the air and landing upside down with me inside, sure to end my suffering. Or maybe I just wanted to hurt myself so that someone else could bandage my wounds—someone to take care of me so I wouldn't have to be big and little at the same time.

My car didn't get a scratch. Not a dent. Not a bump. The curb stopped my little car dead in its tracks. And I screamed.

And I cried.

29

Cast Out the Darkness

I never again tried to hurt myself, though I often wished I was dead. I wished God would end my pain and grant me peace, yet I was afraid of death. In college, I tried to be perfect so that I could someday merit the rewards of heaven, escape the fiery depths of hell, and see my mom again. I set daily goals to read the scriptures and exercise and serve others, especially my family, and work and study and pray. I smiled and said "Hi" and went to church. I organized a sub-for-Santa program and worked as a volunteer for a group trying to raise awareness for the handicapped. I taught piano lessons and read stories to Annie and read my scriptures and set more goals for improvement because I wasn't yet perfect. I tried to *will* myself to perfection. On December 30, 1980, I wrote in my journal:

> *I must not be mediocre, but rise above . . . by climbing the ladder one step at a time. I can't bypass any steps, but I can run. But I must take time to notice the sunsets and my little brothers and sisters as they grow up. I must be a good example to them. I must have control of my life. Control of everything. Control of my temper. Control of my eating habits. Control of my time. Control of my thoughts. Control of my emotions. Control of my spirituality. Control of my passions. Control of myself.*

This is what life is all about, I thought. *Controlling myself. I must learn to control my body—or why else would I have a body?* I couldn't control my mom's death, so I set about to control myself.

I ran miles every day. One day I ran nine miles with Cary. I tried

149

fasting to lose weight and repulsed myself when I ended my fasts with a dozen chocolate chip cookies or a bag of cheese puffs. I vowed to fast again the next day to make up for the junk food I had downed. I read and memorized scriptures. I tried to feel the light and wrote about faith and Jesus Christ and heaven and hope—hope that I could be good enough to make it to heaven.

On November 23, 1980, the month after my eighteenth birthday, I wrote:

> *Lately I've been thinking about getting married, and there's one reason why I'm excited to: I know my mom's going to be there, and I'm going to know that she's okay. I love her so much, and sometimes I miss her a lot, but I'll see her again sometime if I'm faithful.*

I dreamt of marriage with each boy I dated—and there were many—fantasizing that all would be bliss when I finally found an eternal companion . . . or when I got to marry the eternal companion I thought I'd already found in my high school sweetheart—the sage who told me Mom wasn't in hell, the boy who I thought about every time I kissed someone else but who left for a two-year mission and asked me not to wait for him. I didn't.

I hadn't waited even before he left. While he was off trying to find himself, I, of course, thought I had already found myself—because I was big even when I felt little. So I jumped from boyfriend to boyfriend. I loved. I wanted to be loved like Mom had loved me.

Or maybe I needed to love and protect and take care of others like I'd taken care of Annie. Jane didn't let me take care of Annie anymore.

When Jane packed me up and moved me out while I was in California between my first and my second years of college, she made it clear that she was done with me. She tossed out my treasures—my pants that I ripped sliding down the Alps of Switzerland the year after Mom died, my Europe journal, and the shoes that still carried the names of the friends I left at the airport when I said goodbye. She boxed up my dolls—the Swiss, Mexican, Betsy Ross, and Hungarian Madame Alexander dolls that Mom had given me, as well as the white angel doll that Kathy gave to me the day after Mom died—and buried them in the cold, dark basement. Jane tried to resurrect the dolls when the basement flooded, but the clothes were already ruined. Shoes and socks were missing. The life was gone. They would never again be perfect.

But I hoped to perfect myself—to wash away my sins and mistakes through the sweat of my own efforts. I slept just four or five hours each night so I could have time to jog and read my scriptures and memorize Shakespeare and write in my journal and do my homework and go to my classes (except when I didn't) and visit my friends and date and audition for plays and write letters to friends who were away on missions or college and go to work—and did I mention read my scriptures and pray? I set goals to pray ten or twenty minutes every day, as if by checking it off the list, praying would secure my place in God's kingdom.

My busyness crowded out the darkness and shielded me from the depression I easily fell into. I was surrounded by people at school, work, and church, but it was hard, with my tightly wrapped heart, to fully connect with others. With my mask firmly in place, I observed myself talking and laughing and loving—but I was acting. I analyzed everything I did against the standard of perfection commanded by God and required by my now immortal and perfect mom.

One early fall day after I returned from California and unloaded my car in the apartment Jane had chosen for me, I walked from one end of campus to the other in the sunshine—and I felt only darkness. The leaves were just beginning to change colors on the majestic mountains to the east. Fall flowers celebrated life with their open blossoms of yellow, orange, red, and purple. Throngs of students danced past me with renewed energy, life, and excitement at the start of a new school year. I longed to share in their palpable happiness.

"Hi," I smiled widely. I looked each person I passed straight in the eye, trying to connect, but a thick blanket of darkness separated me from the light around me. With each smile I shared, a snake tightened its slithery body around my throat and whispered in my ear, "You are dark. You are stealing their light." I tried to ignore the snake's death grip and continued to smile. After all, my mask was firmly in place.

The snake whispered again. "You are dark. You are stealing their light." He spoke as if the very act of me living was sucking away the breath and life from others.

My eyes blurred. I could no longer see faces. Instead, I saw ghosts. Devils. I gasped for air. The snake's grip tightened. I would surely die.

I wanted to run, but the darkness followed me—swarms of ghosts and dark spirits attacking and invading.

I walked faster and faster to escape. I ran inside the religion building on campus and looked for someone who could give me a priesthood blessing and cast out the demons that haunted me. It was late in the afternoon, so the building was empty. After trying several locked doors, I came to one room with a light on. Seeking protection, I entered the room.

The gentleman at the desk, Brother Pace, invited me to take a seat. Through my tears, I explained, "I feel like I'm stealing other people's light!"

I felt possessed by Satan. In my self-imposed quest for perfection, I noticed my every imperfection, and the snake would not loosen his hold on me. He tried to squeeze every last breath from my existence. I looked to Brother Pace to save me from certain destruction.

Brother Pace firmly placed his hands on top of my head, and with power from God, he pronounced a blessing. "In the name of Jesus Christ," he said, "I command the adversary to leave you."

As he said these words, a dark swarm of unseen beasts exited up my esophagus and out my mouth. There seemed to be hundreds of light-stealing intruders that had invaded my very being.

My tears flowed freely. The snake was sucked away. I was released from Satan's grasp, and a sliver of light returned—a sparkle that danced on my tearstained cheeks.

30

Angels in the Night

Mom had always wanted to play the piano. One summer, Mom took us back east to visit Grandma and Grandpa while Dad stayed behind to finish up some work. He planned to meet us later in the trip. Dad knew that Mom wanted a piano, and he decided to surprise her with one on our return. He carefully chose a simple but beautiful upright piano that was discounted because of a broken leg.

Mom was ecstatic. She lovingly polished the light golden-brown finish each week and dusted it daily. Mom loved piano music. She drooled over Liberace and took me to his concert when I was six years old. Mom enrolled me in my first piano lessons that same year and planted in my mind the idea that I could be as good as the sparkly, diamond-studded performer. On my way to fame, I wrote my first song at age seven.

Although I loved the piano, I hated practicing while my friends rode their bikes outside our living room window. While rehearsing finger scales, I would stare at the flat round timer Mom had set for forty-five minutes. *Only fifteen minutes? It feels like forever!* I often thought as I watched it count down minutes that seemed like hours. Sometimes the timer ticked so slowly that I would give it a nudge and take off five or ten minutes of the remaining time.

Mom came to all my recitals and bragged to her sisters about how good I was. By the time I was in junior high, I no longer needed a timer. I *wanted* to practice. I wanted to play. I dreamed of becoming a concert pianist, and I practiced my favorite songs over and over again until they were perfect.

After Mom died, the piano became my escape. I played for hours and hours, transporting myself to heaven on the wings of the notes to look for God, angels, or Mom. I imagined Mom listening to me as I played her favorite songs, including "Que Será, Será" from *The Man Who Knew too Much*:

> *Whatever will be will be;*
> *The future's not ours to see . . .*

Mom never did take piano lessons herself, though music filled our home. Mom had a beautiful but untrained soprano voice. She rehearsed primary songs with us during weekly family nights and unashamedly sang out with the congregation each Sunday during church. She encouraged me to sing the hymns by her example.

On the day of Mom's funeral, her friend Connie sat on the back row of the chapel listening to hymns meant to comfort. Connie looked up and saw an angel—Mom—sitting at the organ joyfully playing alongside the accompanist. The music Mom had learned in the heavens long ago had returned to her heart. Her fingers were loosed once again to play the celestial notes.

"Your mom would be so proud of you if she could see you now and hear you play," Aunt Grace said one day while I played the piano for her. I wished Mom could hear me, but I wondered if she ever would. Still, I played.

I played for friends. I played for church. I played for recitals. I played for myself.

I played for my husband to-be-while he sang Carol Lynn Pearson's "Angel Lullaby" to me:

> *You came from a land where all is light,*
> *To a world half day and a world half night.*
> *To guide you by day, you have my love,*
> *And to guard you by night your friends above.*

This simple song became a favorite in our family. Mark sang the comforting words to each of our babies after they were born.

> *There's one standing softly by your bed,*
> *And another sits close with a hand on your head.*
> *There's one at the window watching for the dawn.*
> *And one waits to wake you when night is gone.*

So sleep, sleep—'til the darkness ends—
Guarded by your angel friends.
So sleep, sleep—'til the darkness ends—
Guarded by your angel friends.

Mom's piano was a centerpiece in our home after Mark and I married. I played with babies at my feet pressing on the pedals. I played with toddlers at my side pounding on the keys next to me. I played while school-age children sang primary songs during family home evenings. And I played while those same children—my children—sang solos for their high school vocal competitions.

After playing for my family for many years, I was asked to play the organ for our church congregation of more than two hundred people. I had never turned down a church assignment before, so I said yes. Since I had never played the organ before, I took a few lessons to learn how to turn it on, set the stops, increase the volume, and pedal the bass notes of simple songs.

As the Sunday when I was to play for the first time approached, I practiced late into the night in the empty chapel to make sure I could move my feet to the right pedals while my fingers played the right notes. I sat on the hard brown bench at the organ in the silent chapel, my feet dangling in front of me like a little girl learning to play the piano for the first time. I adjusted the bench so my feet could reach the organ pedalboard, and I placed my hands on the lower keys. I increased the volume with my right foot and began to clumsily play one of my favorite hymns, "The Spirit of God."

Unlike when playing the piano, there is no room for error with an organ. It doesn't matter how softly you play—if you hit a wrong note, the entire congregation hears. I was determined to learn the piece perfectly, but with both feet and both hands I stumbled to wrong note after wrong note.

"Slow down, Wendy," I said to myself. My hands knew the song by memory, but my feet couldn't keep up.

After several hours of slow, methodical, painstaking practice, playing one measure to perfection before moving on to the next measure, I tried to string all the measures together at tempo. My hands and feet got all twisted up and stumbled awkwardly across the keyboard and the pedals.

Exasperated, I extended my fingers and dropped my flat hands on the keyboard. I held onto the discordant chord like a child throwing a tantrum.

"Help!" I said out loud. "I need to learn this song tonight!"

I removed my hands from the keyboard and looked at the clock. It was well past dinnertime, and the windows above the chapel were already dark. My back hurt, my fingers were stiff, and I wasn't ready to play the song in the morning.

I said a silent prayer and begged for help. As if in answer to that prayer, I instantly thought of Mom. My heart opened. My fingers were loosed. The chapel filled with warmth, and I felt Mom take her place next to me on the organ bench.

31

Mom Lives!

Keep scrubbing," John reminded me as I stood to leave. He escorted me down the hall and out the back exit to the bathroom so I could wash the streaks of mascara off my face. With my mask removed, I looked in the mirror and saw nakedness—a face etched with decades of silenced grief and unspeakable sorrow. I cried some more while I scrubbed at the dark stains under my eyes and on my cheeks.

Breathe, Wendy. Breathe. Stop crying! You'll ruin your makeup again. I put on fresh lipstick and dried my red eyes one more time. *Please don't let me see anyone I know,* I thought as I hurried off the elevator and out the closest exit.

At home, I spent the entire day mourning. *I can't find any pictures of Mom! Where is my baby book?* I frantically searched through box after box in our storage room. *Where is a picture? I can't remember what she looks like!* Panic built in my heart.

What did she look like before she died? How can I remember her? I need to see her! Mom, where are you? I need you!

Sobbing, I pulled a birthday gift bag Dad had given to me a couple of years earlier down from my top closet shelf. I reached inside and carefully removed the dusty tissue paper I had left in place to protect the contents. I carefully grasped the cool, soft, silky material on top and unfolded the antique white temple gown. Delicate lace accented the high collar and the cuffs of the arm-length sleeves.

How tall were you? I asked through my tears. I held up the long dress in front of me. *I'm taller than you, Mom.* I smiled to myself. *And bigger.*

I imagined talking to my mom. I imagined looking into her face—the face I could no longer see when I closed my eyes and couldn't see now with my tear-filled eyes wide open.

I pressed the dress to my face in hopes that I could smell Mom—her perfume, her body, anything. But, no, the dress just smelled old. Musty and old like mothballs. Her scent was long gone. Not even a hint of Tabu on the discolored collar below where Mom's chin rested as she bowed her head in reverence in God's holy temple. I touched the collar that I'm certain still carried a piece of her DNA. I longed to feel Mom, to touch her, to hug her.

"Mom, I love you!" I said out loud. I gathered the silky material in my arms and hugged the empty dress to my chest. I pressed the gown to my lips and kissed Mom. Instantly, I felt a surge of light. Electricity passed through me—Mom's energy. Mom. Pure love touched my heart and filled my body with shivery, goose-bumpy warmth. Mom's soul embraced mine.

"Mom, I love you. I love you!" I cried as I wrapped myself in her gown. I pressed the white angel gown to my lips and kissed Mom again. Her arms still surrounded my heart. Mom's heavenly light pierced through the dark clouds of despair and filled my heart with healing love.

Mom was alive! She was somewhere. I could no longer doubt that, but I missed her terribly. And although I couldn't deny her loving arms around me as I hugged her heavenly dress, the deep sadness I carried with me remained in my heart.

With greater resolve, I determined to remove the debris that buried my heart. I determined to discover all I could about Mom's life—and her death. All I could think about was Mom. I wrote in my journal on March 18, 2011: "I can't put the lid on. I don't want to put the lid on—I want to be fixed."

I watched home movies. *Mom was alive!* I smiled when I saw her vibrant, youthful energy and her radiant smile. She was always in a hurry. And so thin! Did she have an eating disorder? I vaguely remember Mom telling me once that it would be good if I threw up all the sugar I had just eaten to get it out of my body.

I called my cousins to learn what they knew of Mom's life and death. One cousin shared that her dad theorized that someone killed Mom. Her dad was troubled that there wasn't a police report and thought there was a cover-up. He thought maybe the body had been moved because there wasn't much blood at the scene.

I called Dad.

"Dad, why wasn't there an investigation into Mom's death? Could it have been an accident? Could someone have killed her? How did you find her? Where was she lying? Where was the gun?"

I wanted details, and Dad shared. After years of silence, Dad shared openly.

"I woke up to a phone call from Larry at the preschool. It was about seven-thirty in the morning. He wanted to talk to your mom, but she wasn't in bed. I went to look for her. I opened the bathroom door and found her dead on the floor. Face up, her head between the tub and the toilet, her feet toward the door, like she had been thrown back from the force of the gun—the gun lying on top of her.

"My military training flooded over me. I immediately grabbed the gun and opened the bolt to make sure there were no other bullets so no one else would get hurt. Then I stood it in the corner.

"I locked the door so you kids wouldn't have to see her lying there, dead on the floor in a pool of blood, and I ran to the bishop's house."

"Why didn't we hear anything, Dad? Did she use a pillow?"

"No. She was just in her nightgown. Her pink nightgown." Dad continued recalling the scene as though it just happened yesterday.

"Could it have been an accident? Could someone else have pulled the trigger?"

"No. The bishop called the police chief, who was in our ward, and asked him to come over. It was clear it was self-inflicted. She leaned over the gun, and the bullet made a hole in the ceiling. We repaired that before you kids came back to the home."

Dad recounted the details of Mom's death with a distant sadness. "She had laid out Annie's clothes for the next morning."

Even in the depths of her darkest and final hour, Mom loved her children. One of my best friends recalled Mom standing behind the backstage curtain watching as I performed in the youth play the night before her death. Was she saying a silent good-bye all those years ago, a good-bye I never heard?

And now, decades later, as Mom wrapped me in the light of her spiritual wings, she still watched me from behind the curtain—the veil that separates mortality from immortality. This time, though, instead of a silent good-bye, her message was heard loud and clear: "I love you, Wendy. And I'm *here!*"

⚘ ⚘

"It's called exposure therapy," John said after I reported my efforts. I felt I *had* to search. I was compelled by an unseen power. I had watched home movies. I had read Dad's memoir and scoured through Mom's *Treasures of Truth*. I had talked with family and friends. I had even talked with Dad. I couldn't stop. I could no longer be silent.

John explained that there was nothing he could do in therapy that would compare with what I had intuitively done on my own—what I had been led to do.

"But I don't want to be crazy," I told him. "I can't think while I'm at work."

"This is the most important work you can be doing right now, Wendy. This is where I want you to focus. People heal from talking."

I told John about the sweet reunion at Uncle Bob's funeral and the love I felt for and from the family I hadn't seen for years—Mom's family. I told him of the heavenly experience of Mom's silky white dress, of feeling her light, her spirit, her warmth, and her love that encircled me as I caressed the gown.

"You have to wonder about your Mom's role in all of this," he said. "She wasn't there to mother you then, but maybe she's trying to mother you now."

The timing of everything was indeed remarkable. It was like it was orchestrated by heavenly hands.

"Wendy, I think you're in the middle of a spiritual experience. People are helping you on both sides of the veil."

I couldn't deny God's hand in my life. Light returned one ray at a time as God helped me remove even the tiniest pebbles. Rocks that were too heavy for me to continue to carry began to be lifted from my heart by angels—guardian angels. My angel mom.

32

Buried Treasure

Each rock that was removed revealed a still-raw wound. Excruciating pain that flooded over me in waves I could no longer control and no longer wanted to control. Tears came easily, and I let them come.

I could think of nothing but Mom. Discovering Mom became my single focus; learning of her life and her death became my passion. I wanted to remember. I wanted to feel. I wanted my two selves to become one, made whole by the love of a Savior who can take away all pain because He felt all pain. He took our pain on himself because He loves us. He loves me. I knew that in my head, but I needed to know it in my heart. So I followed where I was led by an unseen hand.

⚜ ⚜

MARCH 26, 2011

"Dad, do you remember a testimony meeting we had sometime before mom died—a family home evening where we recorded our testimonies?" I asked Dad over the telephone.

"No, I don't remember."

"I had a flash of memory today. I was sitting on the bottom stair of our family room and looking across the room at Mom lying on the black couch. She was bearing her testimony into a microphone. Would you still have that tape?"

"I don't know. I don't remember it, but I can look. Why don't you come up to the house tomorrow? I can show you the pictures you asked about, and I can look for the tape before you come."

"Sounds good."

After church the next day, I drove by myself up the winding mountain road to Dad's home, which sat on the side of the road, surrounded by big pines and quaking aspens. The dining room window looked down on the little gray cabin that had been red when Mom was alive.

Jane enthusiastically greeted me at the door, saying that Dad had spent hours going through boxes of photos and other memorabilia. He looked forward to sharing them with me.

Dad had lined up the boxed treasures in the small sitting area at one end of the family room, organized so he could walk me through the contents—his prized memories of Mom.

For four and a half hours, Dad sat next to me on the two-person couch and opened box after box. He opened a scrapbook Mom had filled with black-and-white photos of their early years as teenagers in love secured to black paper with antique photo corners. Mom's beautiful inscriptions, handwritten in white, described each priceless memory.

Dad had discovered Mom's big, round gold-framed glasses. I smiled when I remembered Mom getting her first pair of glasses after Drew was born. "There are leaves on the trees!" she exclaimed in delight.

Dad opened another scrapbook—Mom's white *Treasures of Truth* binder. Its pages were filled with memories of her youth—report cards, school photos of herself and her friends, golden hair clippings, pictures of her teen idols cut from old magazines, and even a rare picture of baby Linda.

Each box Dad shared contained a piece of Mom's short earthly life—a letter to her dad, a Fathers' Day card, a newspaper clipping about her volleyball team, a high school yearbook.

Finally, Dad removed a legal-sized blue vinyl photo album with yellowed see-through pockets that held a handful of pictures.

"Have I ever shown these to you?" Dad asked as he opened the album.

My heart stopped momentarily, and I gasped as I looked at Mom in a pink-and-bronze casket lined with satin. The raw pain of a twelve-year-old's loss flooded over me as I sat next to Dad nearly thirty-six years later.

"No, Dad. I've never seen these," I said quietly. "She was so young."

We were all so young. Baby Annie danced on a neighboring head-stone in one picture, and little Drew knelt on the cemetery grass in another. Marie stood in front of the pile of flowers carefully arranged over a freshly dug grave and smiled for the camera like she had been taught to do by Mom.

"I feel bad that Cary's not in any of the pictures," Dad said.

"I just watched the home movie that Uncle Richard took the day of Mom's funeral, and there's a shot of Cary with a camera around his neck. Cary must have taken the pictures."

"Maybe so."

Dad arranged many of the treasures in a box for me to take home—pictures, newspaper clippings announcing the marriages and deaths of Mom's relatives, her glasses, and even her *Treasures of Truth*.

"I found this tape. I don't know if it is the one you're looking for," Dad said as he handed me an old Certron 45 cassette tape. Dad's faded handwriting on the goldenrod label read, "Testimonies—Family Night."

❄ ❄

"Testing. testing, one-two-three." Dad's commanding voice thrust me back in time as I listened to the tape back home in my bedroom. Why this tape survived intact when so many treasures had been discarded over the years I could only attribute to divine providence—the same providence that had lifted a buried memory of a young girl to the front of my mind.

Annie babbled enthusiastically in the background of the tape. She let out an occasional cry or shriek, drowning out all other conversation as she voiced her displeasure at being restrained on a lap. The microphone scratched loudly with the slightest wiggle, distorting the words of the person who was sharing, as Dad described, "How you feel about your family and the church"—their testimonies, or beliefs.

After Dad made sure the old cassette player was capturing his own voice, he handed the microphone to Marie. Young, bright, seven-year-old Marie's innocence sparkled through her words of allegiance to her parents, family, and church. "I love my parents and my family 'cause they're nice to me," she said. "I know that sometimes I have to get spankings 'cause I'm . . . they want to teach me what's right. I hope that our family can be much better and I know that we can be loving and I know that the church is true and that we love each other."

"Now is it my turn?" four-year-old Drew questioned.

"Uh-hum," Dad replied. "How do you feel about the family, Drew?"

"I want you to hold me."

"Alright. How do you feel about the family, Drew?"

"I feel g-o-o-d." Drew held onto the word. He spoke his sweet, tender truths into the microphone. "I like the church. And I like my family."

Over the whispers of the three other children and Annie's impatient cries, Dad instructed Drew to close his testimony with, "In the name of Jesus Christ, amen."

I sat alone on my bedroom floor and watched the tape wind round and round. The words transported me back thirty-six years to March 31, 1975, the day this priceless treasure was recorded. It preserved the innocence of a young, rambunctious family sixteen days before their world darkened.

I tried to capture every word, every sound, every whisper of this busy young family to which I belonged. I strained to hear any evidence of Mom's participation underneath the loud crackle of outdated technology. My ears were met instead with the thunderous boom of a powerful dad who demanded obedience—a dad who tried to demonstrate how to share our innermost thoughts and feelings about our church and family, yet scared us with his commanding presence.

"I want to tell you kids how important it is that we function as a family unit," he said into the microphone. "We must learn to appreciate each other for the good points and overlook the bad so that we can all become better people, so that we can stay together as a family."

He was attempting to bring us together, but I had cringed from fear of reprimand. "We have a problem in this family, and it's probably my fault," he continued. "And that problem is that we are selfish," he said with emphasis. "Each one of us, from the very head of the family to . . . even Annie has selfish tendencies," he punctuated.

"How come it's your fault?" Cary questioned.

"I'm not saying it's my fault. You kids have minds—"

"You said it's probably your fault," Cary interrupted.

"You kids have, uh, minds of your own," Dad countered.

"Then how come you said it's your fault?" Cary pressed.

"Because I haven't set a very good example in some things, have I?!" Dad snapped impatiently.

"No," Cary responded.

"So we all need to improve, and we need to help each other," Dad continued.

I listened as Dad described how we should be better so we could earn our place in heaven. My childhood fear of Dad returned.

But still I listened.

After Dad said "Amen," I heard whispers in the background. Drew vied for Dad's attention while a young Wendy—a young me—giggled underneath the pop-pop of the microphone.

"Um," my little voice said.

"Be close if you're going to talk," Dad commanded.

"What am I supposed to say?" I whispered. My high-pitched voice trembled with a nervous flutter that I released with a giggle.

"How do you bear your testimony?" Dad reprimanded. "Say what the spirit—"

"Okay, um." I started loudly as I mustered courage. "I'm thankful for our . . . for Mom and Dad and everything they help me with and, um, I know that sometimes I expect too much from them." I spoke in hurried phrases separated by short, apprehensive, awkward pauses, complete with a rural western twang that I outgrew after Jane became my dad's new wife.

"And I'm, uh, thankful for brothers and sisters, and, I'm . . . Marie and Cary and Drew and Annie . . . and especially when we can get along, it's lots funner to . . . to do things when you can get along and just enjoy each other's company."

Annie screamed loudly in the background, and Drew said, "Daddy. Dad."

"And I know the church is true, and I'm thankful for the teachers in the ward, Sunday school teacher Brother Morrell, and Kathy, MIA teacher. And . . .. glad to have the opportunity of bein' the second counselor."

"That's all," I whispered under my breath. And I hurriedly added, "Name of Jesus Christ, amen."

I heard my little voice on the recording whisper, "Do you want to go?"

"Cary?" Dad said, encouraging him to take his turn.

"I'd like to hear from Mom first," Cary countered.

I leaned against my bed frame as the tape continued. I braced myself for Mom's voice. I strained to block out the loud crackles of the microphone being passed to my quiet mom holding her noisy baby. My mom had not said one word during the fifteen or so minutes of the structured chaos of a family home evening testimony meeting. Annie screamed, cried, and babbled over and under everyone else's words, but Mom remained silent until Cary had pressed to hear from her.

"I'd like to . . . ," Mom began, a soft distance in her voice. It was a voice I didn't recognize. *I can't hear her*, I thought. I got closer to the stereo speaker and turned up the volume just to be met with a loud screech from the microphone followed by screams from baby Annie, who must have been trying to grab it. Drew talked in the background, negotiating with Dad for some attention. Mom sat silently on the couch while Annie reached for the microphone.

A full thirty-six seconds later, Mom began again under Annie's cries and the scratch of the microphone. "I'd like to . . . " Mom paused while Annie cried and the microphone scratched. ". . . thank my Heavenly Father for the blessings that he has given me." I listened with my eyes closed, trying to block out the loud fingernail-on-chalkboard scratching of the microphone and the screams of a one-year-old who wanted a turn. *I can't hear mom. Is she speaking? What is she saying?* I turned down the volume again and listened even more intently. *I just hear noise.*

"Don't hit her!" Drew said in the background, followed by a whispered "Ow!"

"Why don't you . . . you lie right here, and I'll work on you," Dad said finally to Drew, who had been trying to get his attention. I imagined my Dad rubbing Drew's back. "Work on you" meant work on your back—give you a massage. The phrase came from Mom's interest in natural healers, and Dad had picked up the vernacular. *But where is Mom?*

After another long pause, Mom returned, weary, depressed, and resigned. "I'd like to thank Him for each one of you." Mom sniffled. *She's crying*, I thought. Drew and Dad still whispered in the background.

"And . . ." Mom cleared her choked-up throat. In my mind's eye, I looked across from my place on the bottom stair of the family room, and I saw Mom lying still, hardly moving—too weak to console a fussy baby. I saw Mom cry.

"I'd like you to know that I know the church is true." Annie cooed in the background, and Mom continued. "That there are many things that we can . . . that we need to do in order to be good members of the church."

Mom paused again. Annie took the opportunity to interject her own words. "Ah-ah-ah-Dad!" Annie babbled loudly. It was a stark contrast to the heavy mist that smothered Mom's quiet words.

"And it begins with . . . being loving to one another . . . and not just to me and to Dad, but to each other." Each word she said was deliberate and panged. She pleaded with her children to be better. She pleaded with her children to love.

"And I pray that we can, each one of us, strive more diligently to be like our Savior wants us to be." She spoke slowly, from a distance many miles away even though she was just across the room.

After another long pause, Mom concluded almost in a whisper, "And I say these things in the name of Jesus Christ, amen."

Annie let out another long scream as Mom handed the microphone back to Dad.

"I'd like to bear my testimony, and . . ." Cary paused. "Maybe not," he said through his own tears.

Cary couldn't continue. Although just ten, Cary had understood the weight of Mom's message. His spirit was touched by her plea to love like the Savior loves.

He began again.

"I'd like to bear my testimony and . . . I know the church is true, and I'm thankful I can be in genealogy class and that I'll be able to get along farther and getting my ancestors better. And thankful for my mom and dad and all the hours they have spent with me. And, and uh, sometimes I sass back and give back talk, but I don't really mean ta hurt their feelings, and . . . I'm thankful for the house we live in and . . . thankful for all the opportunities I have and . . . and, uh, thankful that I can go to church and . . . and . . . um, thankful for the pets I have and my sisters, even though I don't get along too well with them, and my brother. And . . . and I say these things in the name of Jesus Christ, amen."

Annie again screamed loudly for her turn, but Dad took the microphone from Cary.

"Okay, Marie, I turn the time back to you, honey," Dad said.

Then silence. I let the tape play and sat in silence, which was suddenly interrupted by young Cary singing, "America, America, let us tell you how we feel. You have given us your treasures, and we love you so." This was followed by an energetic "Jeremiah was a bullfrog, na-na-na, was a good friend of mine!" I smiled to myself and remembered fearless Cary sneaking the tape player out after our family home evening to record these immortal songs—buried treasures lost long ago but now uncovered by angel hands.

I decided to make a recording of this priceless tape for each brother and sister and my dad as Easter gifts. *Maybe someone can erase all the distractions so we can hear her better.*

I grabbed a pen and some paper and rewound the tape to the beginning of Mom's testimony. I began the painstaking task of transcribing the words I could barely make out underneath the microphone pops, baby cries, children's giggles, and Dad's whispers.

"And it begins with . . . being loving to one another . . . and not just to me and to Dad, but to each other." I stopped the tape, rewinding it over and over again to capture and transcribe each word. "And I pray that we can, each one of us, strive more diligently to be like our Savior wants us to be." More than an hour later, I had scribbled Mom's final "amen."

What was it Mom just said underneath Annie's screams? I rewound the tape and listened again as Mom handed the loud microphone back to Dad.

"They weren't . . ." I couldn't make out the last word. *They weren't what? What did Mom say?* Dad answered with a long "No," and his voice trailed off.

I rewound the tape again and concentrated even harder at blocking out Annie's screams. I was back on the bottom stair looking across the red shag family room carpet at Mom lying on the black couch. "They weren't listening," she said as she handed the microphone back to Dad. "No," dad replied.

"They weren't listening," I heard Mom say. I heard her, and I remembered. I remembered her disappointment. I remembered her pain. I remembered the sharp guilt I felt fueling my desire to be better—to be better for Mom. To listen.

Mom, I'm listening! I cried. My heart overflowed with love. Love not only for Mom but also for each of my brothers and sisters, who two weeks and two days later woke to a silent, motherless, ghost-filled home—brothers and sisters who obediently poured their tender souls into a crackling microphone and sealed their desire to be better, their devotion, and their love in Jesus' name.

I hear you now, Mom. And I'm listening! "I'm listening, Mom!" I said out loud.

I prepared five handwritten letters to accompany the digitized recording of the old tape, as well as a typed transcript of Mom's testimony for each of my siblings and my Dad. *I'm listening*, I thought as I resolutely penned my own testimony. Feelings leapt from my newly uncovered heart—my feelings about a Savior who comforts and teaches and heals and loves. A Savior of light. A Redeemer. A Savior who lifts from the darkest abyss, even from the depths of hell. A Savior who died so all might live—so Mom might live.

"I'm listening, Mom," I said to myself as I prepared this Easter gift thirty-six years after the tape had been recorded. My written words inadequately expressed the love that spilled from my heart for my brothers and sisters and my Dad. Love comes from God himself, from His gift to us—His Son! It was love that I had kept buried for too long in a heart I'd been trying to protect with rocks and dirt.

I'm listening.

33

I Needed a Savior

I would love to talk to Swen," I told Marie on our way home from lunch with our cousins. "He could tell us how Mom died and how he found her. He could tell us about the police investigation."

Marie and I had spent the afternoon with cousins Gina and Katie, Mom's sisters' daughters who were a few years older than I was. They had both attended Uncle Bob's funeral the month before. I hadn't seen most of my cousins for many years prior to that, but I felt drawn back home to these women who forty years earlier had reluctantly let me tag along with them down the Santa Cruz boardwalk and, guitars in their hands, into a magical recording booth much like the room behind the curtain in the Wizard of Oz.

"Imagine me and you—I do. I think about you day and night. It's only right to think about the guy you love and hold him tight, so happy together!" We sang, and the booth etched the music onto a vinyl record. We were on our way to stardom.

I loved these ladies. Mom was leading me to reconnect with them, to discover new things, to heal my heart, and to love others.

Gina's dad, Uncle Carl, had been the one troubled by Mom's death. Although he had died several years earlier, Gina remembered bits of his suspicions. Mom was like a daughter to Carl. He took her under his wing after Mom's own mom died when she was seventeen. Carl was devastated by Mom's apparent suicide. It couldn't be that she'd taken her own life. Carl researched and investigated and hypothesized about the events. He visited the police department and asked to see the police report only to find that there wasn't one.

Trying to make sense of the insensible, he'd tried to piece together what happened. He theorized that maybe someone else shot her. Maybe it was an accident; maybe someone moved the body; maybe there was a cover-up. He said there was hardly any blood in the bathroom. If she had shot herself in the bathroom, there certainly would have been more blood, he said. He was especially troubled to learn there was never an investigation and pointed the finger at Dad for orchestrating a cover-up. And indeed, there had been a cover-up, but not the kind that Carl had imagined. The cover-up involved an oath of silence: protect the children from the truth.

"I think I know where Swen lives," Marie said. Swen was the police chief who came when the bishop called thirty-six years earlier. "He lives close to me. I saw him watering his plants in his front yard the other day."

"Let's go knock on his door," I suggested. "He would be able to tell us what happened."

I felt like the investigator now, though I was a bit nervous for my first interview. With pen and paper in hand, we knocked on his door.

We were greeted by a tall, robust, handsome gentleman originally from Denmark who came to the United States with his family when he was just a boy. He had retired from his police work sixteen years earlier and had since buried his first wife and a son. His thick, wavy, once-blond hair was now silvery gray, but he carried with him the same warm confidence I remembered from my youth.

"Hi, Swen," Marie said, "I don't know if you remember us or not . . ."

"Oh yes, of course. Come on in." He invited us to sit in his comfortable living room while we divulged the nature of our visit.

"We're doing research into our mom's death," I said, "and we wondered if you'd be willing to answer some of our questions."

"Of course. That was a tragic time for all of us," he began. "Especially for you children. Now, when did your mom die?" he asked for a frame of reference.

"April 16, 1975."

"Hmm," he thought for a moment, "I was a new chief of police. I started the year earlier, in February 1974."

For the next hour, Swen recalled the details of his involvement as if it had happened yesterday.

"The bishop called me up and told me what had happened. He asked if I could come over. We were concerned about you children and wanted to make sure the bathroom was cleaned up before you returned home."

"Could it have been an accident? Or could someone else have killed her?" I asked.

"No. I don't remember reading an autopsy report, but it was pretty cut and dry."

"There wasn't an autopsy done," I interrupted.

"Nowadays there's always one done with unattended deaths," he answered. "It was clearly self-inflicted, though. She leaned over the rifle and shot herself. The bullet went through the ceiling. My brother helped me patch the hole."

"Where did she shoot herself? We were told she shot herself in the stomach, but it would have taken a while for her to die if it was her stomach, wouldn't it? And wouldn't there have been lots more blood?"

"She leaned over the gun and shot herself in the chest," Swen began, "with a rifle. The exit wound was much larger—in the middle of her back. There really wasn't much blood. You don't bleed when you're dead. There was more tissue than blood.

"I remember the tissue," Swen continued, "because I asked my wife to come and help me clean up the bathroom. She was quite upset by it. She took the bath rug to our home to wash it. Some of the tissue got stuck in our washing machine lint trap—tiny pieces that she had a hard time getting out. It disturbed her."

"What an incredible act of service," Marie said somberly. "An angel."

"I can't even imagine how difficult it must have been," I added.

"Yes, it was especially difficult for her. I had seen things like that before in my line of work, but she hadn't. It was an awful thing—very hard. But we were concerned for you kids and wanted to make sure you didn't come home to it."

"Did anyone else help you clean the bathroom?" I asked.

"No, I don't remember anyone else there with me except my wife. No." He paused for a moment reflecting. "I did go into the basement, though, and talked to a boy—I thought he was maybe a young teenager."

173

"My brother, Cary?" I asked.

"It must have been your brother."

"He was ten," I said.

"He was on the stairs in the basement. I told him what happened—that his mom had died. I remember how difficult that conversation was. How do you tell a young boy that his mom is dead? Difficult." Then Swen asked us a question. "Did anyone hear the gunshot?"

"No, we were all asleep. No one heard anything." Marie and I both responded.

"I'm surprised that no one heard the gun go off. It would have been very loud. Those rifles, fired in an enclosed space, are very, very loud."

"I woke to my dad's frantic cries," I said. An angel must have protected five small children and a sleeping dad from the thunderous boom of the rifle. How else did we sleep through the unthinkable?

"Did any other police come?" I questioned.

"I don't remember any other police. It was handled as a ward thing. I came over when the bishop called," Swen said. "I didn't really see myself as acting as the police chief, but I must have been. We all just tried to protect you children."

"Yeah, we didn't know how she died. Your son is the one who told me," I said with a half-smile.

"He did? I'm sorry. I'll have to get after him for that." Swen matched my smile.

"Other kids said that she died in the bathtub in a pool of blood," said Marie. "My dad kept me out of school for a long time so I wouldn't hear the gossip."

But she didn't die in the bathtub in a pool of blood. It wasn't an accident. She wasn't murdered. She stood in the middle of the bathroom in her pink nightgown, leaned over the gun—a hunting rifle aimed at her chest—and pulled the trigger. The force of the shot thrust her backwards to the ground, her head between the tub and the toilet, and blew open a gaping hole of shredded flesh—tissue on the bathroom rug that an angel neighbor washed in her own washing machine.

Mom took her own life and died instantly. No second chances. No cries for help.

And we were all left to ask the question, "Why?" We can do our best to put together the pieces and to hypothesize the reasons like my uncle did, but in the end, after this life is finished, only God can tell us why. Only God can heal our hearts.

Pieces of my own heart were shredded that same day, left on an invisible bathroom rug, unable to be washed away except through the atoning blood of a Savior who carries all heartaches, whose own wounded hands I was beginning to see. As I uncovered my heart and let His light penetrate the open wound, I knew it would one day be healed by His love.

34

God Sent an Angel— God Sent His Son

"Marie, have you been able to sleep?" I asked at a breakfast get-together with her and Aunt Leslie.

"No! All I could think about was tissue."

"Me too! The tissue that got stuck in the washer freaked me out."

"What?" interrupted Aunt Leslie.

We explained to her that we had met with Swen two days earlier on our quest to discover Mom. I was grateful for Marie's willingness to accompany me on this painful journey.

Aunt Leslie had worked with Mom at the movie theater before either of them was married. Mom introduced Leslie to Dad's next oldest brother, Robert, whom she married a short time after Mom married Dad. Robert and Leslie had lived on the street just south of ours when Mom died. They moved away shortly after Dad remarried. Although Leslie faithfully accepted each invitation to baby blessings and wedding receptions, I had never talked with her about Mom at length. Now she'd agreed to look to the past and reminisce with us about Mom over breakfast.

Aunt Leslie had arrived at the restaurant a few minutes early—at least, earlier than either Marie or I had—dressed in a beautiful, pressed, cream-colored linen dress. Quiet, reserved, and proper, Leslie had married into Dad's loud and boisterous family. She relied on Mom's energy and youthful determination to help shield her from the often offensive culture of her in-laws.

Mom and Leslie had talked nearly every day on the telephone. They talked about everything—kids, husbands, what they would do when they grew old, and so on. The long phone cords of the day allowed access to nearly every corner of the house.

"Your mom moved so fast and got so much done, running through the house in her bare feet while she talked on the phone all day long," Aunt Leslie remembered, smiling. "One day I went barefoot like your mom, determined to get my whole house cleaned. But I couldn't do it. All I did was hurt my feet!

"She loved to laugh. She was so happy and had so much energy and was so much fun to be around. I loved her laugh. I loved your mom! And she loved you children." Aunt Leslie spoke softly now, intent on relaying the message in her heart—Mom's message.

"I wasn't really able to sleep well last night either," Aunt Leslie said. "I lay awake wondering what I would tell you. I prayed to know what your mom wanted you to know. I prayed to know what to say."

Tears filled her eyes. "You need to know that your mom loved you. She loved you with everything in her heart. She loved you!"

Mom loved us. She loved me! The message was clear. She spoke to my heart at Uncle Bob's funeral; she touched my soul when I hugged her white temple gown; and she whispered to me when I listened to the once-buried testimony tape.

But if she loved me, then *Why*? And *How*? How could she purposely destroy her body? How could she leave her five children? How could she leave a baby? How could she pull the trigger?

"She wasn't the same after her cardiac arrest," Aunt Leslie continued. "She didn't have any energy. Everything was so overwhelming for her—the house, the kids, church. Your mom was very angry at your dad for commanding her back. She'd wanted to die then."

Dad had explained how Mom became even more spiritual after her near-death experience—wandering off to talk to angels unseen by earthly eyes. But Aunt Leslie added that Mom saw other beings too. "After her heart failure, your mom saw evil spirits. I tried to encourage her to get your house blessed, but she would just hit them away."

Evil spirits bent on dragging Mom to hell, I thought. And yet the questions remained—*Why? How?*

At home, I searched on the internet for any more clues. What happens when you kill yourself, I wondered? Were there any near-death experiences of people who had purposely shot themselves? How did tiny Mom reach the trigger while leaning over the barrel? And why?

I looked up rifles. The British .303 that Cary said Mom used had a 25-inch barrel and was 44 ½ inches long in total. It would have been nearly impossible for her to reach the trigger. Dad said that it wasn't the British .303—it was the Winchester .270, a bit shorter at 42 ½ inches total length with a 22-inch barrel. That made more sense. That gun was the perfect size if you were five-foot-two and aiming for your chest.

What was going through your mind, Mom? How could you do it? Did you die instantly? Did you have any final thoughts—thoughts of your children? Did you have any last regrets as you fired the deadly shot, flew backwards, and hit the floor? It was too late by then.

Surely the loud blast must have violently shaken the small bathroom and masked the thud of her lifeless body. But what masked the boom? Even the blasts on the internet hurt my ears. They penetrated my heart and shook my soul. *How did we not hear her?*

I clicked through page after page of hunting rifles and googled exit wounds. I stared at the large hole ripped in the hide of a bear and thought of Mom's lifeless, broken body . . . and the tissue that clung to the inside of a washing machine.

Just like our good police chief's wife had tried to wash every bit of bloody, broken flesh from our bathroom rug, I tried to wash the shredded pieces from my heart. Some of the pieces stuck. No matter how many tears I cried, salty water wouldn't release the pain. And I lay awake at night, afraid of a bang I'd never heard.

✂ ✄

"John, I can't sleep. All I can see is blood—the blood splatters on the shower curtain. I can't wash them away," I told him in therapy one day.

"We could try some EMDR to process this trauma."

EMDR, or *Eye Movement Desensitization and Reprocessing*, is a treatment used with soldiers returning from war as a way to speed up healing from post-traumatic stress disorder. From researching EMDR, I learned that the therapy stimulates a REM-like state as the patient focuses on a traumatic event and simultaneously follows a finger or a wand back and forth with their eyes, listens to a tone alternating from ear to ear in a headset, or holds onto paddles that alternate short vibrations from hand to hand. During this REM-like state, unprocessed traumatic memories can be released and moved from memory storage sites in the brain such as the limbic system (the emotional fight-or-flight center), to the prefrontal cortex, where those memories can be reprocessed and made bearable.

I was ready to speed up my healing. I no longer wanted to see blood when I closed my eyes. I took hold of the small paddles John handed me. As he'd instructed, I closed my eyes and thought about being in the tub and discovering the speckles of blood on the shower curtain.

I held my breath, nervous about what I would see. As the paddles began vibrating, I saw fragments of memory. I stepped into the tub, naked and alone. I pulled the curtain. I saw the blood. I froze in place, too terrified to move. I shivered from cold. My legs shook uncontrollably as I sat on the couch in John's office. I opened my eyes and slowly came back to the present. I told John what I'd seen.

"Wendy, you *were* alone and vulnerable. Nakedness symbolizes that vulnerability. Your body shook because of the memories stored there— muscle memory from that traumatic event. It *was* cold. You *were* naked. You need to release those memories as part of the reprocessing."

John helped me understand the experience. He gave me courage to look, see, and heal. "You didn't have anyone to run to back then, to protect you, to help you process what you had just seen. So now we get to reprocess those painful memories and make meaning of them."

At home, I had more flashes of memory. I saw my twelve-year-old self sit in the tub and pull the curtain. The blood splatters stared at me, five inches from my face. My breath wouldn't come. I hid behind the curtain, unable to move. Was I next to be murdered? When I finally lifted myself from the tub, I dripped on the rug and saw more splatters—brown ones on the wall by the baseboard next to the tub.

I replayed the scene over and over in my mind, allowing myself to look at the scary details. Because I hadn't processed Mom's death when I was twelve, I had carried disabling fears with me my whole life—fears of heights, medicine, spiders, snakes, and germs. Fears of cars crashing and rocks falling. Fears of strangers, knives, ropes, and especially guns. Fear of the dark. Fear of ghosts. Fear of death. Fear of hell.

I opened my eyes, my mind, and my heart, and I looked. I trusted

John, God, and angels. And Mom. Somehow, by looking—by allowing the fear to rise to the forefront of my mind—its intensity diminished. It was imperceptible at first, but still I looked.

When I returned to John's office, I again grabbed the vibrating paddles and closed my eyes to see.

※ ※

"John, I had an incredible experience this past week as I meditated on the bathroom," I told him one day. After several EMDR sessions filled with blood and ghosts and horror, I had begun to move through the fear and embrace meaning. *Installation* is what John called it—pairing the positive with the painful.

I knew Mom, on God's errand, was encouraging me to look—to see not only the visible but also the invisible—to see that which is unseen to earthly eyes.

After my appointment with John, at home alone in my bedroom, I closed my eyes. And God opened my mind.

I saw myself sitting in the tub, seeing the blood splatters, and getting out of the tub completely naked, my wet hair dripping on the floor. Then I saw Kathy come in and wrap me in warmth—a towel and a robe. She touched me. She loved me.

I cried and said, "My mom is dead. She can see everything." My nakedness represented my nakedness before God and my mom.

I was hysterical, but Kathy comforted me. I tried to blame myself for my mom's death. "If only I was better. If I had been good . . . I should have been able to stop her."

Kathy reminded me that it wasn't my fault and that Mom loved me more than life itself.

"Then why did she shoot herself? Why?"

"Because she was sick. But she still loved you, and Jesus loves you."

Kathy warmed me. She pushed the hair out of my eyes so I could see.

She cleaned off the blood splatters on the wall, the shower curtain, and the cupboard. The bathroom sparkled. She told me she loved me and that the Savior loved me.

And then I saw the Savior.

Kathy became the Savior—His wounded hands touched my face. He'd blessed me through Kathy, but it was the Savior the whole time. He took my face in His hands, and I looked at Him. His loving eyes warmed me. But I looked at the wounds in His hands, touched them, and then I knew for certain that they were there for me.

He cleaned the wall, and the room became bright white. I saw all the angels that were there supporting me through that awful experience. The angels of my past—my family.

My mom was there. I argued with her about how bad I was, and I cried. I said, "I'm sorry," and she forgave me and loved me.

Mom was there, and so was Grandma Florence, Grandma Eva, Grandpa Rowley, and their parents—generations of angels who loved me. I saw my cousins and my aunts Carol, Grace, and Mary. The room opened to the heavens, yet its dimensions remained the same. The room was crowded with angels. They all saw my nakedness, and they loved me anyway.

It still is crowded with angels. And they will always love me.

I saw myself as a grown-up—my own age—take that twelve-year-old in my arms.

And then I saw myself touch my twelve-year-old heart, and I saw the Savior help me take out the bullet lodged there. I was his assistant in surgery. We had forceps or some sort of surgical tool, and we took out the bullet. There was a big hole in my heart, and the Savior touched it and it filled with golden green light. He filled it with love from the bottom up, and he handed me this perfect, pink beating heart to return to myself. I placed it back in my twelve-year-old self's chest and hugged her.

The room filled with light, and my spirit filled with light, and I knew that I wasn't alone as a twelve-year-old girl and that I'm not alone now.

And I knew that I needed to share my story.

And I knew that I needed to love.

I lay on the floor of my bedroom and I sobbed. God hadn't left me alone in my darkest hour. Just like to Jesus in the Garden of Gethsemane, God had sent me an angel. God sent a multitude of angels to a twelve-year-old girl who sat alone in a bathroom surrounded by blood. God sent his son, Jesus Christ, my Savior and Redeemer, to wipe away that blood, take away the stain, and make the room sparkle with a light brighter and whiter than I could comprehend with my earthly eyes. God sent his Son to take the bullet from my heart and fill the hole with healing light—to fill my heart with love.

35

Angels on Earth

Marjean was one of the earthly angels God sent to rescue five abandoned children from the dark abyss of unimaginable grief. *Where
was Marjean now?* I wondered. *What would she remember?*

Again, Marie agreed to accompany me to visit Marjean and her
husband, Ron, the bishop to whom Dad had run when he first found
Mom on the bathroom floor. Marie and I hesitantly approached the
front door of a home that stood on a well manicured yard. When we
knocked, Marjean cheerfully greeted us and welcomed us into their
warm, inviting home. Ron had recently suffered a stroke, and his
memory was not as sharp as it once was, but Marjean had hardly aged.
At more than seventy, Marjean still found the time and energy to do
Zumba.

After catching us up on who was who in their big family portrait,
Marjean invited us to sit with her and Ron around a kitchen table
spread with all sorts of goodies. Marjean had comforted us with forbid-
den treats once before—when she'd led five small children from the
haunted home where our dead mother lay, and fed us ice cream for
breakfast.

"I heard screaming, wailing at the door. I thought it sounded like
someone was laughing, but it was your dad. He was hysterical," Marjean recounted. "Your dad was grieving the most immense grief that
was humanly possible to bear and still live."

I thought of Dad, the firm, commanding man I feared—the man
who seemed to demand perfection. I thought of his sadness, his grief,

and his immense pain at seeing his wife lifeless on the bathroom floor, her flesh torn from her body by a bullet aimed at her heart. His own heart must have broken that day too.

Your dad was grieving the most immense grief that was humanly possible to bear and still live, I repeated in my mind. My heart filled with love for Dad, who for the past thirty-six years had held his family together the best way he knew how—sometimes with shredded bandages, but with eternal commitment nonetheless.

"You'll never know why," Ron said when he handed us copies of the funeral address he'd given thirty-six years earlier to a congregation of more than a thousand. Ron had saved that address for all these years. It read, in part:

> *Walt, I join with your friends, neighbors, and family in offering our love and support.*
>
> *Last evening after the viewing, you mentioned to me how, as the line of visitors moved forward, each person you met offered you added strength. Indeed, each who has been in your presence these past few days has felt your power and faith. Moments after the tragedy Wednesday morning, Walt gathered his children around him, and as we kneeled together, Walt pled for understanding, faith, and support. He then arose in control and with strength. We who have come to comfort have been comforted.*
>
> *As Linda's bishop, friend, and neighbor, I have come to appreciate her many beautiful qualities. I think of her sparkle and her zest for living. She was full of life, and her enthusiasm and bubbling personality positively affected all in her presence. She was active and athletic and loved to go to their mountain home to enjoy its warmth, its serenity, its inspiration for family closeness, and its natural beauty.*
>
> *She had much to give and did give of herself freely and unselfishly. Was she close to the Lord? Her life pattern attests to her devotion, her love of her Heavenly Father and His Son, and to her knowledge and testimony of the truthfulness of the Gospel.*

Ron shared with the congregation those many years ago the testimony Mom had penned while recuperating after her cardiac arrest:

> *To my family—thoughts I have had this day:*
> *There is no shortcut to perfection. Step by step we will progress to the top honors and rewards our Father in Heaven has in store for His children. This task is a great one—but we must remember that where*

much is given, much is expected. We can't get all bogged down in trivia, so much that we lose sight of our goal—that of eternal life. We must realize that this is our top goal. Along the path of life there will be many small and large goals for us to achieve—our first school play or our first talk in Sunday School—and as we progress, our first piano recital or dance review, cub meeting, etc. The list could go on and on and will, but remember that as we anticipate each of these steps in our lives, we must always be mindful of our great responsibility to ourselves and to our Heavenly Father—to act our very best and do our very best whatever it may be, so that we can return again to live with Him—because He loves us so very, very much and longs for our return when our mission and trials in this life are over.

Love each day and each new challenge. We will continue to grow in strength physically and spiritually if we are ever mindful of the many, many blessings that are ours because we have such a kind, loving Father.

I will close this letter today with my testimony. I bear witness that the things I have written are true—the gospel is beautiful and true. My prayer at this time is that my family will know for themselves of the truthfulness of these things and work diligently, along with me, to this end that I speak of, namely, eternal life—and that of making our call and election sure while yet in this life. For these things I pray in Jesus' name, Amen.

P.S. Remember, one step at a time is enough for me.

Ron's address continued:

These past months have been difficult for Linda and Walt and their family. No one else will ever know the pain, the struggle, yet the hope for a physical and emotional recovery.

None of us can hope to understand fully the workings of another's mind, spirit, or soul. Thus, only to our loving and merciful Father in Heaven is given the right and power to understand and judge.

Walt, may our Savior's life and the purpose of His death and resurrection have added meaning to you and your family . . . In the writings of Paul, we read, "If in this life only we have hope in Christ, we are of all men most miserable." With trust in divine providence, all who are faithful will in due course be brought together in Christ. Encouraged by this hope, may our fears be subdued and our troubled souls find peace and reassurance.

For most of us here today, our hearts are heavy—some are troubled, some feel guilt, some are confused, some afraid. Long ago, the Savior, near his death, gave His apostles a blessing, which may be appropriately extended to each of us here today: "Peace I leave with you, my peace I give unto you: not as the world giveth, give I unto you. Let not your heart be troubled, neither let it be afraid."

"She loved you," Marjean said. "Your mom loved you."

36

Guardian Angels—My Angel Mom

SUMMER 2011

"John, I feel angels around me," I exclaimed in therapy one day. I'd been riding my bike out of the city and to the mountains every day. John had instructed me to do healing activities between our sessions, and cycling was one of the things that filled my soul. My mind could wander from past to present to past again while I cycled next to the river on the tree-lined pathway that stretched from Utah Lake to Vivian Park.

One particular day toward the end of summer, I rode to the end of the trail and sat on the shore next to the river. The trees bent toward the water's edge and cradled me in their long branches. I was removed from the world and transported to heaven in my mind as I watched the water roll musically down the mountain, never stopping to catch its breath, endlessly, effortlessly moving forward. I thought of Mom, and my eyes filled with tears. I wished that I could move forward effortlessly. *Mom, it's so hard! I miss you!*

The sun seeped through the spaces between the leaves and danced on the ground. In that moment, in the warmth of the fading summer light, the branches reached down to encircle me. Heavenly beings surrounded me and touched my heart. God's angels embraced me and loved me. I was not alone.

I was never alone.

And now, Mom accompanied me on a life-changing journey. A painful journey, full of buried rocks and dirt, but also full of treasure.

Mom took me by the hand as I looked in all the dark corners of my heart. Angels lit the way—angels of my past, grandmas and grandpas and aunts and uncles long since gone from this earth, and angels of my present placed in my life by the hand of God, who directs all life.

"I know I'm being protected, John, I know it's going to be okay."

The journey wove through my darkest days—a blood-stained bathroom, a forever-closed casket, and the rocks and dirt of a buried, silent past. And God sent his light—love that wrapped around my unburied heart and began to heal even my deepest wounds.

"How's your anger?" John asked. It was a barometer of the therapy I'd begun months ago.

"I don't feel anger. I don't feel like two people anymore."

As the light shined on my darkest hours, I saw my imperfect mom, who took her life so that she might escape her own darkness. And I felt God's love penetrate my unburied heart. What pains, griefs, guilts, and sorrows had Mom kept buried, hidden from the world, covered with her own rocks? Her rocks eventually buried her.

And yet, she still lives. Her light reaches down from heaven to touch her children.

"I don't believe in coincidence," John said. "No experience is wasted on God. He can take the most painful, awful situations and make good come from them."

Good can come from a broken family, a broken life, a broken home, and a broken heart. Because of our darkest of days, we realize our complete dependence on God our Father and His Son, Jesus Christ. In humility, we cry to Him in our bedrooms. We cry to Him in our closets. We cry to Him in the mountains and the fields and the dungeons of our earthly existence. I cried to Him in my bathroom. We look toward heaven through our tears. And in the quiet moments of our despair, after all our tears are spent, when we can no longer utter a prayer and we fall silent on the ground, then we can listen. And by listening, we learn that our Savior can take our broken selves and make us whole. He can heal our broken hearts.

"But John, I can't fix it," I said as I reprocessed some of the many mistakes I had made as a child. I was afraid of the judgments that surely awaited me for my hidden mistakes that would be made visible in the hereafter. "I can't make it right."

I held onto the vibrating paddles and closed my eyes. I saw Mom. She took me by the hand to heaven. She tenderly pushed my hair out of my eyes so I could see. I asked her, "But how can I fix it?"

"You can't," she said matter-of-factly. I cried, and I knew she knew. She knew the deep regret of unfixable mistakes better than I could ever know. She knew the pain of my heart, and she knew she could never fix it. She could never make it right. None of us can ever fix it. We can't take away the pain of our mistakes—pain inflicted on others or pain that others inflict on us. We can't fix it.

"But the Savior can," Mom continued. "The Savior can make it right. He can fix it. Your job is to love. Open your heart and love."

In that moment I saw my Savior, my brother. I saw Heavenly Father and countless angels. I saw Marie and Cary and Drew and Annie and Jane and Dad and Sally and Grandpa Rowley and Grandma Eva, and generations past and future all wrapped in the glorious love of God.

My job was to open my heart and let the Savior fill it with light. My job was to love. That's all—just love.

Mom did love me. She was there. I felt her by my side on God's errand, guiding me and protecting me. She could love me because the Savior loved first. And because the Savior loved first, I could love.

We all have a story—hidden secrets buried in dark and rocky earth. Our journey is to unearth the pain and discover the good, discover the healing, and discover the love—to uncover the darkness and make space for the light.

Epilogue

Mark, I don't know where I am. How do I get to Central Park?" I asked from two thousand miles away, cell phone to my ear as I exited the cramped hotel onto the crowded New York City sidewalk. The swift current made it impossible to stand still for fear of drowning in the deep river of people hurriedly walking to work or shops or theaters.

I had arrived by myself in this bigger-than-life city after conducting a survey for a hospital a couple of hours away. I extended my work trip so that I could visit the city, which I'd last seen on my way to Europe the year after Mom died. Upon arriving the day before, I made my way from the expansive bus stop and awkwardly dragged my suitcase and computer bag down the escalator and out the door. I felt instantly ant sized. I craned my neck back as far as it would go to find the tops of the giant concrete buildings towering above me.

Back home, Mark stayed close to the computer to help me navigate the foreign streets of this gigantic city using the Internet. With my luggage safely stored in my tiny hotel room and my phone to my ear, I asked Mark to guide me through the crowded streets.

"Turn left and walk to Fifth Avenue," Mark said.

"Where's Fifth?" I asked, clutching the small purse draped over my shoulder.

"It's the next street."

"And then where do I go?"

"Are you on Fifth yet?"

"Not yet. Just a few more buildings to the next corner."

191

"When you get to Fifth, you'll turn left and keep walking. You'll eventually run into Central Park."

One of millions of people, I trotted to keep up with the lively current. "Okay, I'm at Fifth," I said. "I'll call you if I get lost. I love you!"

I was alone again in the sea of people.

I smiled at the street vendors. A tie for Mark would be his only souvenir. A pretzel and water for me. *Seven dollars?!*

"Will you take a picture for me?" I asked the man standing by the lion in front of the New York Public Library. I entered the magnificent building held up by massive Greek pillars. I marveled at the art and architecture of this center open to the masses.

I wandered past stores. Some were in our mall back home, and some weren't. I even made my way into the diamond district I had heard about. My eyes weren't big enough to take it all in. I ate lunch in the Trump Tower and sat and watched mothers and children delight in the fountains of the Rockefeller Center. A kind gentleman offered to take my picture by the just-blooming tulips that lined the manicured walkways.

What is that building? I asked myself as I made my way back to Fifth Avenue after exploring the Rockefeller Center. I was drawn to the castle buried between the skyscrapers that filled the streets. I had visited Notre Dame in France and a few other cathedrals in my youth, but I was unprepared for what lay behind the massive bronze doors of St. Patrick's Cathedral.

When I entered the cathedral, I was immediately struck by the reverence that encircled that holy place. From the busy New York City sidewalk, one can enter it and be removed from the world.

My tears flowed freely as I walked the perimeter of the expansive chapel. From the brilliant stained-glass windows to the life-sized statues and paintings that lined the walls, this cathedral testified of the One who came to heal the world. I witnessed, as if for the first time, my Savior, my brother who carried his cross to Calvary.

My heart full to overflowing, I entered a pew and knelt to offer a silent prayer. I had never prayed in such a public place before, but I couldn't stop the words flowing from my heart. I prayed in gratitude that someone as unworthy as I was could be redeemed from pain and sorrow, heartache and sin. I could be saved. And if I could be saved, surely my mom could be saved.

Jesus paid the price. He willingly offered Himself a sacrifice for me. He offered Himself a sacrifice for my brothers and sisters and my dad and Jane and Grandma and even my grandpa. He offered Himself a sacrifice for all who had lived. He offered Himself a sacrifice for my mom, who had died during her darkest time. He offered Himself a sacrifice so that she could be brought into the light of His love.

Ant-sized, I knelt there in that giant cathedral and offered my prayer. God heard, and he touched my heart with a finger as brilliant as the burning bush on Sinai. A light enveloped my soul.

I lit a candle for Mom in that cathedral—a candle to carry my prayer to heaven. And although the light of Mom's earthly candle was extinguished before the wick had burnt to the plate, her heavenly light lives on eternally. She watches over me—on God's errand.

Acknowledgments

When I first learned that I was unable to return to work after the bicycle accident, I was devastated. An electrical storm raged in my head. I couldn't read or look at a computer screen or remember how to get home when I walked out of church a block away.

I had always prided myself in my ability to think and reason, and now my neuropsychological evaluation showed that I had severe memory impairment. My nursing career was over. In my now silent and darkened world, free from the noise of distraction or work, God spoke to my heart, and I could finally listen.

Writing the story of my mom's suicide would be my new work. Without knowing the end of the story but trusting that God did, I picked up a pencil and wrote, sometimes just a sentence or two, in my spiral-bound notebook.

Two years later, there was no more to write. I had not read my own manuscript—reading was and still is difficult—but I felt impressed to connect with Lee Nelson. He felt, as I did, that together we could make a difference. If there was just one life to be saved by me telling my healing journey, then I must unashamedly share my truth. I am grateful to Lee Nelson and to the entire staff at Cedar Fort who took a chance on an unknown author with a broken brain. Thank you to the wonderful editors who transformed the story into a beautiful piece that could be shared with the world.

Thank you to the many angels on both sides of the veil who accompanied me on this journey. My angel friends Janelle and Melissa read each chapter as I wrote it and listened without judgment as I shared the thoughts and feelings of my heart. Barney gladly took my manuscript and offered his editing expertise, reminding me to show, not tell. Lisa helped me see the unseen angels guiding this work. And my massage therapist Mindee, herself a suicide survivor, helped quiet my brain and taught me the importance of healing from the inside out.

I am forever grateful to John, my inspired therapist, who believed my story. He believed I could heal. He helped me uncover the layers and open my heart.

Thank you to the cousins, aunts, uncles, and friends of my distant past who welcomed me with open arms after my many years' absence and helped fill in the gaps in my memory. I ask you to forgive me for any unintentional inaccuracies in telling Mom's story. And thank you, Aunt Leslie, for reading through your own tears and pain and giving me the courage to tell the truth despite my fears.

Thank you to those friends of my more recent past—my MBA classmates who willingly offered their marketing talents and skills to help me reach those who hope for healing after devastating loss. Without your support, these pages would have stayed hidden behind a book cover.

My siblings each have their own story to tell, yet they allowed me the space to tell mine and still loved me. For that I am grateful. I love you each dearly.

Heartfelt thanks to my stepmom, who encouraged me to write. Although she has struggled with her own mental illness, she chose to live! My life is richer because of her influence.

Thank you to my beautiful daughter, who painstakingly helped me format my manuscript for submission when my brain no longer wanted to work, and to my three sons, who offered blessings and prayers on my behalf. I am blessed with amazing children who, despite my shortcomings as their mother, have grown into beautiful, giving adults. Although unworthy, I am grateful for your never-ending love.

Mark, I am eternally grateful for your sensitivity, your compassion, and your unselfish charity. You supported me in my darkest hour and gave me strength to seek the light. I cannot imagine my life without you by my side. I love you forever.

Words are inadequate to express my gratitude to you, Dad. You held together our tattered family. I am amazed at your ability to live through such heartache, thrive despite adversity, and still believe in God. Thank you for reading words that tore at your heart and for loving me anyway.

Mom, my guardian angel, thank you for teaching me about a Savior who heals all wounds, who wipes away all tears, and who loves without condition. Thank you for guiding me to the light.

About the Author

Wendy Parmley suffered a disabling bike accident in September 2011. Unable to return to her twenty-year nursing career because of the continued effects of her injuries, Wendy began the slow and painful penning of her angel mother's story and her own healing journey following her mom's suicide. Wendy's mom took her own life at thirty-one years old, leaving behind her husband of thirteen years and their five young children.

Wendy has long advocated for suicide prevention and has participated in various professional and community-based groups dedicated to that end. She also recognizes the need to unashamedly support those who must continue to live in the painful aftermath of a loved one's suicide and passionately lends her voice to that cause.

Prior to her bike accident, Wendy worked in nursing leadership for fourteen years, earning her MBA degree from Brigham Young University in 2007. Despite her continued limitations, Wendy is grateful to spend more time with the love of her life, her husband Mark. She is ever grateful for his support and the support of their three married sons and their wives, their amazing daughter, and their two beautiful grandchildren, who fill their life with sunshine. Mark and Wendy live in Orem, Utah.

Mental Health Resources

National Suicide Prevention Lifeline

1-800-SUICIDE (1-800-784-2433)
1-800-273-TALK (8255)

OR

www.suicidepreventionlifeline.org
1-800-799-4TTY (4889) for hearing impaired
Dial 2-1-1 for local support or www.211.org
UNI CrisisLine (Utah)
1-801-587-3000

American Foundation for Suicide Prevention

https://www.afsp.org/
http://www.mentalhealth.va.gov/
http://www.nami.org/
http://www.mentalhealth.gov/

0 26575 15006 3